A Surgeon's Life
With Bipolar Disorder

This book provided a lot of interesting information and insight into bipolar disorder and other mental illnesses. A Surgeon's Life with Bipolar Disorder is a book about hope; ideal for a wide range of a reading audience.

—PACIFIC BOOK REVIEW

A Surgeon's Life
With Bipolar Disorder

John A. Emery, MD

Copyright © 2019 by Author's Name.

ISBN-978-1-6455-0675-1

All rights reserved. No part of this book may be reproduced or transmitted in any form or by any means, electronic or mechanical, including photocopying, recording, or by any information storage and retrieval system, without permission in writing from the copyright owner.

The views expressed in this work are solely those of the author and do not necessarily reflect the views of the publisher, and the publisher hereby disclaims any responsibility for them.

Matchstick Literary
1-888-306-8885
orders@matchliterary.com

Dedication

To our brothers and sisters with a mental illness.

CONTENTS

About the Author ix
About the Book xi
Introduction xiii

Chapter 1.   Bipolar Disorder 1
Chapter 2.   A Life With Bipolar Disorder 39
Chapter 3.   The Beach Cities Of Southwest Los
              Angeles County 67
Chapter 4.   Ucla 80
Chapter 5.   Ucsf Medical School 112
Chapter 6.   The Tumultuous 60'S 126
Chapter 7.   Internship At Los Angeles County
              Hospital 128
Chapter 8.   House Calls In Los Angeles 140
Chapter 9.   The War In Vietnam 145
Chapter 10.   Vietnam 150
Chapter 11.   Urology Residency At The University
              Of Oregon Medical School 182
Chapter 12.   Private Practice 201

Index 253

About the Author

Dr. Emery was born in Niagara Falls, New York. He grew up in Charleston, West Virginia. He graduated from Torrance high school in Torrance, California. He attended UCLA with a football and academic scholarship. He attended UCSF Medical School. He did an internship at Los Angeles County Hospital. He was a Navy doctor with the USMC in the Vietnam War. He finished a Urology residency and practiced Urology in Southern California for over 30 years. He has two children and six grandchildren. He previously published a book on US Medical Care and Related Factors in the Vietnam War.

About the Book

Dr. Emery has written this book to enhance your knowledge of bipolar disorder and point out how it affected his life.

He will tell you of some of the unique experiences he has had during his life. These experiences will include his experience with the Watts Riot of 1965, the Vietnam War and the Tet Offensive of 1968.

When appropriate, he will give you his medical perspective on some of these experiences.

We hope you will enjoy the book.

Introduction

Hello, and thank you for sharing this book with me. For some time, I have considered writing a book about my experience with bipolar disorder. I thought that it would be interesting and informative for others to see how one person dealt with this disease.

I have been a surgeon for many years. I was diagnosed as having bipolar disorder at age 39. I have experienced most of the scenarios one can experience with this disease. I hope my description of these experiences and how they affected my life will help you understand this disease better.

I have divided the book into two parts. In the first part I will tell you of what I know about bipolar disorder and how it might affect any of our lives. In the second part of the book I will tell you of my experience with this disease before and after my diagnosis. This will involve telling you about some of the many unique and coincidental experiences I have had. Among these, are my experiences I had in the mountains and valleys of West Virginia, in "the Happy Days'" as they were in the beach cities of Los Angeles, in the UCLA educational, football and Greek programs, with my many unique friends at UCSF Medical School, in the 1965 Watts riot in Los Angeles, in the Vietnam War in 1967-68, including the Tet Offensive of 1968, in my residency in Urology and in the beginning of a practice in Southern California. All of these experiences occurred prior to my diagnosis of bipolar disorder. Since this disease is congenital we may see some manifestations of it in my early years.

During the course of telling you of these experiences, I will place a medical perspective on some of them. For instance, I will use my experience of playing football at UCLA to discuss the problems we all can have while exercising in hot weather. Some of the experiences I had while practicing Urology are very humorous.

Overall this book is just an example of how one person lived a life with bipolar disorder. I hope you will find this book interesting and informative.

Chapter 1

Bipolar Disorder

We all have encountered people with disabilities. With external physical or functional disabilities, the impairments that the person is facing are, for the most part, easy to see. In the case of internal physical or chemical diseases, such as heart disease or diabetes, the diseases are hard to detect, even for the trained eye. With mental diseases, the situation is similar to these internal physical or internal chemical diseases by virtue of the fact that they too are hard to identify. The mental illnesses differ from these internal medical illnesses by virtue of the fact that we do not know of a specific biologic or biochemical abnormality that is causing the mental illness.

Bipolar disorder is likely an exception to this general rule by virtue of the fact it is thought to be a mental disease which is caused by a specific biochemical abnormality in the brain. This defect is thought to be an abnormality of the neurotransmitter system of the brain. I will get more into this chemical abnormality later.

Whether we see a person with a mental or physical disability, let's not forget that there is person in there trying to deal with their disability as best as they can. They are playing the hand they were dealt. They may or may not be able to deal with their disability in a way that we would expect or hope they could. That doesn't mean they are not trying to cope with their disability or there isn't a way that we can help them.

What exactly is bipolar disorder? We know bipolar disorder is a mental disease in which a person experiences abnormally severe swings of emotion. The disease is congenitally passed from one person to another in a family where the gene is present that causes this disease. It is thought that the gene associated with many mental disorders may be on the same chromosome in our DNA. I have family members who have had long periods of depression.

These swings of emotion can vary from severe hyperactivity and euphoria to what can be a severe, prolonged and devastating depression. The disease can "cycle" as rapidly as once every day or more than once a day. More likely, the cycling occurs over a more prolonged period of time. I seemed to have a longer cycling recurrence rate in which I had severe swings of emotion every several (up to 5 to 10) years. For me these cycles were identified by severe depression episodes. This is probably because of the devastating effect these depression episodes can have on your psyche. The feelings created by these depression episodes for me were very traumatic.

I have had three such severe depressive episodes during my experience with this disease. Thank goodness you can recover from these episodes with the help your doctors, medication and time. I had more minor swings of emotion during the intervening years.

Experts tell us that up to 4% of our population has bipolar disease. The disease is a chronic recurrent disorder carrying a high degree of morbidity and mortality leading to a health cost of more than 45 billion dollars per year. It is the sixth leading cause of disability in our society. 25% to 50% of adults afflicted with this disease will attempt suicide at least once during their life. 8% to 18% of adults with this disease will die of suicide.

Early onset bipolar disorder in children and adolescents is much harder to manage than when it is seen in adults. These children and adolescents are extremely difficult to care for.

Their families have an overwhelming task to try to educate them about this disease and have their disease treated well. Unfortunately, these young patients face a lifelong effort to cope with this disease.

Most everyone has "normal" swings of emotion and that is true in the person who has bipolar disorder as well. The person with bipolar disorder, however, can experience extreme swings of emotion that can be difficult to explain to the person who does not have this disease.

I once listened to a Professor of Psychiatry at the University of California Medical School in San Francisco answer the question of how he would explain what bipolar disorder is to a patient or one of his children. He said he would ask them to think of a time when they were most happy and magnify that feeling by a factor of 10 and that's how they would feel in the state of hypomania with this disease.

A similar situation was true on the depressive side of the disease. Think of a time when you were most unhappy or down and magnify that by a factor of 10 and you will see how severe the depressive phase of this disease can be. I certainly would agree with that.

In my experience with this this disease, the manifestations of the disease had to with my gender, my life plan objectives, and my previous life experiences. If you are a female or another male, your experiences will be related to your gender, your character, your direction in life and your previous life experiences. These experiences will be different than mine.

In my experience, women have a greater interest in knowing about diseases than men do. Women feel responsible for the health of their families, they are use to seeing medical providers throughout their lives and they are very instinctive when it comes identifying the onset or presence of an illness, especially in their families. <u>One of the most important adages' in medicine is never to discount the instincts or concerns of a female when it comes to identifying health problems of those close to her.</u>

As noted, those who have bipolar disorder are born with it. One major variable is when this disease will become manifested in their lives. Will that time of onset be early in their lives or will the time of clinically significant manifestations of this disease be later in their lives? For me this disease was diagnosed when I was in my late thirties.

Have these patients shown signs of this disease before it was diagnosed in them? Yes, I think that happens commonly in patients with bipolar disorder. If that were so, do you think that the activities they have engaged in during the subclinical (not clinically significant) hyperactive phase of their disease could account for some of the positive accomplishments the bipolar patient has achieved. I think this an interesting question within the dynamics of this disease. I believe this has happened in my life. Certainly, there were many times when I had a singular and intense focus on the goal I was trying to achieve.

Most people are not aware of people with bipolar disorder who are a part of their lives. The bipolar patient may be a family member, co-worker, or simply a friend or person you know. The bipolar patient is unlikely to discuss this disease with others because of their fear of rejection from family and friends. These patients are aware of the negative connotations this disease generates in the society.

As noted, the disease can manifest itself by hyperactive, erratic and accelerated behavior. This accelerated or abnormal hyperactive behavior can attract the attention of family, friends, the police, the legal system, the press or other people in our society. In this hyperactive (manic or hypomanic) phase of the disease the patient unexplainably goes into a hyperactive type of behavior that is out of context with his or her normal behavior. In such a state the patient is said to be in a manic or hypomanic behavior pattern. Their activities can become erratic and bizarre. The patients may make poor decisions that can put themselves and/or others into positions discomfort or even peril.

The opposite feature of the disease is an abnormally severe level of depression which may, and frequently does, follow an episode of the hyperactive abnormal behavior. This depression phase of the illness frequently is preceded by a feeling of paranoia by the patient. In my case, all of the severe depressive episodes were preceded by a period of paranoia.

The "trigger event" or incident associated with the onset of the depressive phase of this disease can seem very minor or insignificant to others. On the other hand, the bipolar person can focus on this seemingly minor event and blow it up to themselves to the point it where to them it becomes a major event which sets off a bipolar depression.

This bipolar depression is caused by an endogenous (produced within the body) chemical abnormality in the brain of the person. This endogenous chemically induced depression can be much more severe than a "non-chemically induced" depression. It can occur in people who apparently have no problems that you think would cause a depression. They might appear to be doing quite well in their lives when suddenly they are in a severe state of depression.

In my opinion, this "chemical" bipolar depression is more resistant to treatment than the "non-chemical" type of depression. This is probably because the bipolar depression is likely caused by this chemical abnormality in the patient's brain, rather than a "reactive" depression we see in a non-bipolar person. These non-bipolar reactive types of depression episodes are usually more self-limited and respond more readily to treatment than the depression that is part of bipolar disorder. This chemically induced, seemingly uncontrollable, bipolar depression is much more severe, is more resistant to treatment and can even result in an unexplained suicide in what was thought to be a normal person.

You have probably seen or heard of such a suicide in a person who seemed to be normal and apparently was living a happy life. When the onset of this disease is a severe depression, it is an important time in the life of the patient with bipolar disorder. They and those around them are unaware of the fact they have bipolar disorder. Most of these people don't know what bipolar disorder is. Those around them wonder why this person is worrying so much over what appears to be a minor problem. The person becomes withdrawn and does not communicate with those who they have communicated with ordinarily. Be conscious of this series of events and you may save a person's life.

The depression phase of this disease is less visible to other people than the hypomanic (hyperactive) phase of the disease, but also can have devastating and possibly deadly effects on the patient.

Many of the abnormal events that are happening in our society today, criminal or non-criminal, are not uncommonly attributed to "bipolar disorder" in the person involved in the event. This conclusion is reached whether the person has bipolar disorder or not. It seems to be common in our country today to hear people or the press say that a person is probably "bipolar" in trying to explain a person's abnormal behavior or the crimes they commit. This person may or may not have bipolar disorder.

Experts believe that people with mental illnesses commit a very small percentage (3-4%) of violent crimes in our country. This fact is particularly pertinent today after we have seen multiple mass shootings in our society. The feeling is that the person doing the mass shooting is mentally ill. These people are unlikely to be mentally ill. The factors more likely to be associated with them are being male, having a bad experience in the workplace, having had hateful and traumatic childhoods, having been involved in abusive relationships and having violent and revengeful personalities.

The public is far less familiar with the bipolar patients who have sought out treatment, have received appropriate treatment from their doctors or medical care professionals, are taking their medication correctly and are functioning well or even exceptionally well in their lives. Perhaps one of these people is a family member, friend or co-worker of yours and, as far as you know, is having no perceptible signs of emotional swings that are out of the ordinary.

Receiving the appropriate treatment for this disease does not ensure that the patient will have a totally normal life free of these emotional swings. In bipolar patients, there can be times when the proper treatment is "overridden" by the expression of the disease. In other words, despite the fact that the patient is being followed by their physician or medical professional and is taking their prescribed medication, there is still the possibility that the disease may get out of control causing the disease to "breakthrough" the treatment the person is receiving resulting in a hypomanic or depressive phase of the disease.

This scenario of breakthrough resembles a diabetic patient getting out of control despite the fact they a taking their medication appropriately. These out of control episodes are usually associated with stress in the diabetic. The diabetic patient can test their blood sugar and thus be aware that they need to change their insulin level. Unfortunately, there is no chemical test for the bipolar patient to alert them to a change in the expression of their disease.

I have experienced such breakthrough events in my life since I was diagnosed with this disease. I will describe to you these events along with the total experience I have had with this disease later in this book.

Mental illnesses, like any disease afflicting anyone in our society, should be addressed like all diseases we can be afflicted with. The more we understand the possible causes of these diseases and how they affect the person and the people around them, the more we can understand and help people who have these diseases.

Bipolar disorder can occur in prominent high-performing people. Many well-known historic figures, such as Winston Churchill and Abraham Lincoln, are believed to have had bipolar disorder. President Lincoln probably had a unipolar type of this disease. He had repeated periods of severe depression during his life. Despite having to deal with these major swings of emotion, he accomplished tremendous achievements as a leader of our country.

Winston Churchill had periods of depression, yet he also achieved significant accomplishments and great leadership during the time of World War 11.

Some well-known composers have written a symphony in one weekend. They were thought to have been in the hypomanic phase of bipolar disorder. Other people in the world of artistic endeavors have done major works in a short period of time leading us to think they probably were in the hypomanic phase of this disease.

The disease is currently divided into two classifications. In type 1 the disease is manifested by recurrent episodes of depression and at least one documented episode of mania. In type 11 the disease the disease is manifested by recurrent episodes of depression and one documented episode of hypomania (a less severe form of mania). Mania is a word that is used to describe an emotional condition in which a person experiences an extreme state of accelerated mental and physical activity. Hypomania is term to describe a similar state, but of less magnitude.

During this state of accelerated activity (or hypomania) a bipolar person may do things that they would not or may not be able to do ordinarily. Their speech and thinking are far more rapid and expansive than it would be under normal circumstances. They may become grandiose and may do unusual things. They may shop for and buy things they don't need. They may make poor social or economic decisions. This behavior can have disturbing effect on family members, friends, co-workers and the public. In the past, this disease was referred to as "Manic Depressive Disease". This name of the disease was then changed to bipolar disorder.

The chemical changes that occur in these patients with bipolar disorder are not simple or completely understood. We do think that the abnormalities primarily occur in the neurotransmitters in our brains. Neurotransmitters are chemical agents that are responsible for the transmission of information from one nerve ending to another or from a nerve ending to an end organ such as the heart, pancreas, stomach, etc. There are a number of these neurotransmitters, perhaps as many as 7, in our bodies.

Among these neurotransmitters, we think that dopamine and serotonin are the two neurotransmitters that are primarily responsible for the abnormalities seen in bipolar disorder.

According to our current understanding, an imbalance between these two neurotransmitter chemical agents in the emotional centers of the brain accounts for the abnormal states of emotions seen in this disease. I'm not implying that the understanding of this disease is this simple, but it lies within the framework of this concept.

Dopamine seems to act on our emotional center in our brain resulting in good cognition, good memory and the drive to reach goals. The second primary neurotransmitter of our brain is serotonin. 90% of serotonin in our body is located and produced in our gastrointestinal tract. To a lesser degree it is located in our brain. When this neurotransmitter acts on our emotional center it also results in a feel good feeling and has a calming effect in our bodies. It enables us to make good decisions based on logic.

When these two neurotransmitters are in balance we are likely to have a fairly normal experience with our emotions. It is when they get out of balance that the bipolar patient can experience extreme variations in their mood. This out of balance state can be manifested by: a high level of dopamine and a low level of serotonin; a high level of serotonin and a low level of dopamine; a low level of both, etc.

Let me emphasize that the exact deviation or changes in concentrations of these neurotransmitters leading to specific changes in mood or behavior in bipolar patients are not known completely to researchers in this field. Suffice it to say that the changes in behavior of these patients is a manifestation of abnormalities in these two neurotransmitters in the brain. These changes are manifested through the emotion producing portion of our brains. In other words, an abnormality in the neurotransmitter systems of the brain acts on the portion of our brain responsible for our emotions to create abnormal expressions in these emotions.

There are certain drugs that can mimic the abnormal mood swings seen in bipolar disorder. For instance, taking a methamphetamine can result in an abnormally strong feeling of euphoria and a high-energy state, similar the state of hypomania seen in the bipolar patient.

When a person is addicted to an amphetamine-like drug, such as crystal methamphetamine ("crystal meth"), and this drug is of a significantly high concentration in their blood stream they can manifest the same sort of symptoms as the bipolar patient when he or she is in an endogenous chemically induced hypomanic state.

On the other hand, if the crystal methamphetamine is withdrawn or is in a low concentration in the addict's blood stream, one can see some of the behavior characteristics similar to the bipolar patient after a prolonged period of mania or hypomania. This low level of the hyperactivity inducing drug (methamphetamine in the addict or the imbalance of endogenous neurotransmitter chemicals [dopamine and serotonin] in the bipolar patient) seems to trigger off a severe state of paranoia and depression. This paranoia and depression can be as extreme as the hypomanic phase of the bipolar patient's behavior.

Notice when I describe the onset of a severe depression episode I use the word paranoia. There is a reason for that. The methamphetamine addict develops a period of confusion and paranoia when he or she are coming down from a "meth high". The same thing occurs when a bipolar patient goes into a depressive phase of their illness. I have never experienced a severe depression that was not preceded by a period of a strong feeling of paranoia and guilt.

As I mentioned, the event kicking off the period of paranoia, guilt and depression in the bipolar patient may seem quite minor to the bystander, but to the bipolar patients the event can be magnified to overwhelming proportions and induce a severe depression that can have devastating effects on them. I will tell you of such events that I experienced later in the book.

Interestingly, this same pattern of behavior can be seen in an example taken from the Second World War. This example may help you to understand the sequence of events I just discussed.

In the Second World War the German soldiers were given a drug to make them fight with more energy, ferocity and endurance. The drug was called "Pervitin". While on this drug the soldiers were euphoric, hyperactive, had great energy and were able to fight furiously for long periods of time. These soldiers were able to complete great feats of accomplishment during their "Blitzkrieg" maneuvers of the German army.

As you know, the word Blitzkrieg (lighting war) was used to describe the German army's ability to take territory and defeat the enemy with lighting speed as they fought on the westward and eastward facing fronts in Europe. They fought with very high energy and enthusiasm for prolonged periods of time. Their execution of maneuvers was fast moving and precise. The drug, Pervitin, was accounting for their enhanced fighting ability.

The German scientists discovered this drug with the use of "pill patrols". A pill patrol consisted of giving prisoners of war various drugs or combinations of drugs and then making them walk in large circles with heavy weights on their backs in all types of weather. Some of the prisoners died on these marches. The results of these pill patrols studies were carefully recorded, especially in relationship to the duration and effectiveness of the prisoners on these pill patrols to complete these marches. The scientists discovered the prisoners preformed best on a methamphetamine. They named this drug Pervitin.

Once these results were obtained the German pharmaceutical factories produced millions these pills. Hitler's personal physician, Dr. Morell, was instrumental in developing the production of Pervitin. He became wealthy by setting up pharmaceutical factories to produce this drug. German soldiers became addicted to this drug after taking it for prolonged periods of time.

When the drug was withdrawn from these soldiers it resulted in a low the concentration of the drug in the soldiers' blood stream. This low concentration of the drug in the soldier's blood resulted in the development of symptoms similar to the methamphetamine addict's withdrawal symptoms. The soldiers would become very agitated, very confused, very paranoid, very passive, very depressed and useless as fighters. This finely tuned ferocious fighting soldier was turned into a frightened, confused and paranoid person when they experienced withdrawal from Pervitin.

One such example of this happening to the German soldiers occurred on the eastern front of Europe in WW11. The German soldiers were off this drug, Pervitin, because of the fact they had used up the existing supply the drug. They became very agitated, frightened and paranoid. One night they were very paranoid and fearful of an attack by the Russians. They used up all their ammunition that night firing at imagined Russian soldiers attacking their front. The Russians realized this fact and attacked their position the following day. The Germans were low on or out of ammunition and were overrun.

These German soldiers were manifesting the same sort of behavior seen in the methamphetamine addict who was in withdrawal from methamphetamine or the bipolar patient going into a paranoia and depression after a period of hypomania.

Could it be that all three of these people were simply running out of an exogenous (the addict on methamphetamine or the German soldiers on Pervitin) stimulant, or in the case of the bipolar patient, an endogenous imbalance of neurotransmitters in the brain, which resulted in all three of them manifesting the same sort of behavior?

Hitler, himself, may have been a methamphetamine addict. This Doctor Morrell was thought to be a "quack" by the other German doctors. Despite that, he developed a close relationship with Hitler. Hitler had great trust in Dr. Morrell's treatment and kept this doctor close to him during the entire war. Dr. Morrell went with him everywhere. In fact, Dr. Morrell was the last person to leave Hitler's bunker before Hitler committed suicide.

Hitler was given a variety of drugs by Dr. Morrell. One of these was probably Pervitin. Perhaps this was given to Hitler so he could keep up with his demanding schedule or simply to make him feel energetic for the day. Some of the drugs were given to Hitler intravenously. Some other of the chemicals he gave Hitler may have been actually poisonous to humans.

There is a debate among experts as to whether Hitler was mentally ill or simply a very evil man who gained extreme power in his country. In either case, he was given a large number of drugs by a doctor who had a very poor reputation among his colleagues in Germany. These drugs contributed to Hitler's eventual severe decline in health.

An interesting sidelight on this issue is the fact that English soldiers fighting the Germans in North Africa at the battle of El Alamein where taking "Bennies" (Benzedrine) to enhance their fighting ability. The German soldiers were taking Pervitin. Thus, this battle is referred to in some history books as the first "amphetamine battle" in history. There are other examples of this where armies or individuals were given some type of stimulant agent before a battle.

The reason for me presenting this information from the Second World War is to bring up the similarities between the behavior of these German soldiers on Pervitin and the behavior of the bipolar patient as they swing from one emotional state to another.

When the German soldiers started this drug, Pervitin, they reacted similar to a bipolar patient going into a hypomanic state. They were euphoric, full of energy and capable of sustaining focus and energy for long periods of time. They were like the composer who wrote a symphony in one weekend. When the Pervitin was withdrawn from the soldiers they behaved similarly to a bipolar patient going into the depressive phase of that illness. They became agitated, paranoid, very depressed and ineffective as soldiers. These are the exact patterns of behavior I had in the cases when I went from a hypomanic state of emotion into a depression. Although I could develop a spontaneous depression, the depression episodes usually followed a state of hypomania.

Fortunately, no patient of mine ever had a negative outcome from my treatment of them because of this disease. I attribute this fact of good fortune, to the excellent care by my doctors, to my level of education and training and, most importantly, to the grace of God.

My doctors treating me for this disease were excellent. They advised me many times on how to manage this disease.

They taught me how to "listen to my body". Whenever I felt a significant change in my emotional state, I was trained to be aware of it and seek their help.

Lithium was the medication the doctors prescribed for me when I was diagnosed with this disease. This medication dulls your affect and has some significant side effects, but it was effective in controlling this disease. Yes, I had a few breakthrough manifestations of the disease even while I was on Lithium.

After I was initially diagnosed with having this disease, I was able to take nearly a year off from practice. I used that year to learn all I could about this disease. I talked to my doctors extensively and learned how to manage this disease. I stopped drinking alcohol completely. I completed a state of California diversion course. Even though I was not substance abuser, it brought me into contact with doctors who were struggling with the management of other problems.

I have never taken crystal methamphetamine, but I have experienced the effects of a period of hypomania as part of my experience with this disease. The first thing I experienced in such an emotional up-swing was the fact that any sort of minor aches or pains in my joints, back or muscles went away. It was as if my joints, muscles, and back had been lubricated. The feeling was very exhilarating. If the hypomania continued to increase I could feel much more strength in my muscles and more coordination. It was if I had been injected with a chemical agent that had induced a state of physical well-being and mental euphoria. Such episodes came on in a short period of time, usually in a few days or less. When I knew that was happening, I discontinued my practice of medicine and did not resume it until I was normal again.

During one my significant episodes of hypomania (I was not working at the time), I could exercise with more strength and fluidity than normal. For example, I was running along an oceanside park and felt as if I could run forever. I am not a runner by nature, but on that occasion I certainly felt like one. Not only that, while running I began to jump on the top of and over cement picnic tables. There is no doubt that this was a wonderful feeling of euphoria in being able to do this type of enhanced physical activity. I can see how a soldier taking Pervitin would be able to perform feats of physical activity that he could not possibly do without a drug being present in his body. The other amazing thing is that I did not tire easily. I felt as if could continue this extreme form of activity for long periods of time. This activity resembled the German soldier on Pervitin who could complete the feats of accomplishments required by the demands of the Blitzkrieg.

Mentally speaking, I felt a feeling of euphoria. It was as if I thought I could do anything with ease. This euphoria is exhilarating and can lead one to attempt things that they would not consider doing under normal circumstances. It is here where the bipolar patient can attract the attention of law enforcement. Depending on the patient's personality they might try to do something either positive or negative.

On one occasion during a hypomanic episode I was trying to help someone with their car tire. I noticed that this car tire was bald and the wire reinforcing was showing through. I told the car owner that he should not be driving himself or anybody else around on this tire. The man probably knew about the tire and did not want to hear my opinion on the situation. Despite that, I continued to explain to him my opinions on what would happen if he continued to drive on that tire. I was truly making a fool out of myself. He became very annoyed and called the police. Somehow, I got out of that predicament.

Lithium was commonly used to prevent and/or modify the hyperactivity or hypomania phase of the disease. This drug was primarily effective in preventing the up swings of emotion. Patients might be controlled with respect to their incidence of hypomania for long periods of time with the use of Lithium.

Lithium was found to have potentially serious side effects, thus the look for other medications to replace it began. I experienced one of the serious side effects of Lithium, which is interstitial nephritis (a type of kidney failure). I eventually required a kidney transplant. The use of Lithium has been reduced today with the introduction of the use of the anti-seizure medications, such as Lamictal, to control the hypomania episodes in the bipolar patient.

Electroshock therapy has been tried in patients who have severe depression and are resistant to conventional therapy.

The success of this therapy is still being evaluated. I tried an abbreviated period of this treatment and found no benefit for my depression.

I believe the most tragic consequence of undiagnosed bipolar disorder occurs when a person, not known to have bipolar disorder, experiences what may be their first experience with the disease as an extreme deviation of emotion, which can result in their injury or death. Let's say an undiagnosed person experiences a severe unrelenting depression as the first manifestation of their bipolar disorder and commits suicide as a result of their depression. This is the person who commits suicide in the face of what appears to be a happy and productive life.

On the other hand, let's take the example of an undiagnosed person experiencing a hypomanic episode as their first manifestation of their bipolar disorder. In this hyperactivity state they may exhibit extremely bizarre behavior. This behavior can draw the attention of the police. In the worst scenario, the person may be injured or killed by the police because of the patient's apparent threatening behavior to other people or the police themselves. Policemen and policewomen are not trained psychiatrists. They react in a way to protect themselves and the others from imminent threats of injury or death and may injure or kill a bipolar patient by accident.

More typically, the bipolar patient can exhibit a less threating, but still erratic and bizarre behavior. Let's say there is a prominent banker in town who does not know he has bipolar disorder. Over a short period of time he feels better than he ever has in his life.

After work one day he stops at a sporting goods store. He has always wanted to go big game hunting in Africa. He buys a very expensive bow and arrow set to use when he goes on a trip to Africa. Of course, he will need to buy expensive binoculars to see the big game animals there. He leaves the store. Once out of the store he tries his new binoculars out and sees a car accident down the block. He decides to go there to help if he can. He decides he would be most helpful by directing traffic around the accident. It's the least he can do to help out. Because it is a hot day he takes his shirt off and goes out into the street with his tank top underwear shirt on. Soon the whole process turns into a mess. His poor ability to direct traffic is not a minor factor in creating the mess.

The police finally arrive. Here is a guy in the middle of the street in a tank top underwear shirt directing traffic. Beyond that there is a fancy bow and arrow set and binoculars lying on the street next to him. They begin to question him as to who he is and what the hell is he doing there in his underwear shirt in the middle of the street. He says he is a manager of a local bank and decided to help with the accident that happened there. He thought the best way he could help was to direct traffic around the accident until they arrived. They then ask about the bow and arrow lying at his feet. He says he bought it to go big game hunting. They wonder if he means in the local area or some faraway place.

Finally, they ask him to go downtown with them so they can figure out the whole situation. They finally clear him at the station and strongly suggest he see his doctor. Sound ridiculous? With bipolar disorder, this may be just another story of how you find out you have this disease.

A more serious scenario can occur when the police have no reason to believe the person they arrested and the person is put into jail after they are screened. Are they a methamphetamine addict out of control? The person is put into a drug withdrawal portion of the jail. The person may not respond normally to the drug withdrawal treatment. They may continue to manifest the behavior of a person with untreated bipolar disorder. Hopefully, their behavior draws the attention of attendant medical personnel and they will be evaluated by a psychologist or psychiatrist and get the appropriate diagnosis and treatment. If this does not happen this patient may languish for years in our penial system without treatment. Surely, there are many such patients in our penial system today.

It's important to emphasize, again, that this disease is superimposed on one's basic personality structure. This means the disease will manifest itself as a swing in emotion consistent with the patient's basic personality traits. This fact is responsible for the great variety of behavior patterns seen in bipolar patients.

In my own experience a period of a significant hypomania with its feelings of euphoria and high energy was always followed by a period of paranoia and depression. In my case the ratios of dopamine and serotonin concentrations in my brain had probably changed which resulted both the hypomanic and depressive state. There is no way to confirm that the ratios of dopamine and serotonin had changed, but from a clinical standpoint that is the likely the sequence of events that happened.

What was that feeling of paranoia and subsequent depression like? It was very real and very devastating to me as I descended into a severe depression. I was a high preforming surgeon in my community. I was a highly educated and highly performing doctor in LA County hospital during the year of the 1965 Watts riot. I had been in combat (enemy rocket attacks on our base) on several occasions, including during the "Big Tet Offensive of 1968". I had treated thousands of patients and had done many difficult surgeries in my practice.

How could such a person develop such a severe depression that could disconnect him from those characteristics which had been a part of him in the past? When I experienced my first major depression reaction it was painful and overwhelmingly devastating.

The incident that started it was very minor. I thought that one of my patients had developed post-operative bleeding. Actually, he had not developed any significant bleeding. This minor, insignificant event suddenly started a period of paranoia and depression. It started with an overwhelming feeling of paranoia and depression and I was reduced to frightened, easily manipulated and painfully depressed person. I was unable to assert myself in any way and was very vulnerable to manipulation by anyone. The felling would go away somewhat when I slept, but returned very soon after I woke up. I will describe this event in detail later in the book.

In retrospect, I cannot describe with complete accuracy the degree of devastation one can feel at that time. I doubt if the general public realizes the amount of pain and insecurity the bipolar patient feels at the time of the occurrence of such a depression reaction. With this level of depression there is a high level of pain associated with it.

During those depression reactions, it was as if I had completely lost my tried and tested coping skills. I had lost my confidence completely and now had lost my defense mechanisms to fight this feeling. What had hit me and reduced me to this fearful person with complete loss of confidence and belief in myself? I'm letting you in on these feelings to somehow allow you to see the total devastation a bipolar depression event can produce.

It was as if the floor I had depended on for stabilization in so many difficult situations in the past was gone completely out from under me. There was no apparent way I could get my feet under me to stabilize the situation. This was huge shock to my whole being. I was hospitalized with this initial and two other severe depression reactions.

Did my experiences in the Vietnam War have anything to do with the manifestation of this disease in me (i.e., because of PTSD)? I don't think so. You may have an opinion on that question after you have read this book.

A cardinal rule for the patient with bipolar disease is not to make any important decisions when they are hypomanic or depressed. In both of those states the patient can be irrational and can frequently make poor decisions. Such decisions, when made while the patient is in an exaggerated state of an emotional swing, can result in disastrous financial errors or disastrous social decisions. These decisions might have permanent consequences for the patient, their family or friends for the rest of their lives. I certainly made some poor non-medical social decisions when I was experiencing a hypomanic swing in emotion.

When I experienced a significant deviation of emotion, I was able to stop working until I recovered. When I recovered from a hypomanic episode or depression episode I was able to return to practice. I went back to treating difficult clinical situations and doing difficult surgeries as I had been doing before.

I would urge the patient with bipolar disorder to become very good at their job. Become a good secretary, a good brick layer, a good farm worker, a good salesperson, a good pilot, a good designer, etc. This allows you to get right back into a successful and productive type of work after your bipolar episode has been treated successfully or has subsided spontaneously. You won't have time to sit around and ruminate about your disease.

In the medical profession, you have to declare you are being treated for bipolar disorder and explain the treatment plan you are undertaking when you are applying for medical staff privileges at a hospital and are doing clinical patient care. The same is true when you are applying for a state license. In general, states will not limit your license if you demonstrate a good knowledge of the disease and show that you are on a good treatment plan that includes good follow-up by your doctor. I have been a doctor in good standing with my state license since I was diagnosed with this disease. If your treatment plan is good there is no reason that you cannot have a successful career.

Can there be occasions where the fact that you are being treated for bipolar disorder be used against you? Sure, there can. Because of my outspoken and extremely firm attitude on good patient care, at times I came into conflict with some of the doctors around me. When I spoke up on situations that I felt were not in the best interest of good care of patients, I could draw the ire of those doctors. Occasionally, some of these doctors tried to discredit me by stating that my outspoken opinion on patient care was because of uncontrolled bipolar disorder. You will see examples of this happening later in the book. In my experience, these same doctors had tried to discredit, injure or destroy the careers of other doctors in our community. These doctors were part of a small minority of doctors in our country who manifest self-serving interests above good patient care.

I hope you will see in this book that you can continue to do your job despite having this disease. If by sharing my experiences with bipolar disorder brings up some questions you have about this disease or helps you understand this disease better, I will have accomplished my purpose for writing this book.

Let's consider the phenomenon of "self-treatment" of this disease by the patient. Self-treatment means that the patient tries to treat themselves for the symptoms they are experiencing. In the example of bipolar disorder, if the patient is having a depression reaction they may try to treat themselves with a drug that will bring them "up". They may use such drugs as cocaine or an amphetamine to try to elevate their mood. Those patients experiencing a manic state may seek a drug such as alcohol or perhaps marijuana or morphine to bring them "down".

Such efforts to treat themselves will expose them to all the dangers of the usage of legal or illegal drugs in our society. They may accidentally overdose with one of these drugs and kill themselves. They could be arrested and be put in jail or prison because their bizarre behavior or use of illegal drugs. In prison, if they are not diagnosed properly, they may continue to try to treat themselves with drugs which are available there.

If the bipolar disorder is diagnosed correctly and early enough in a person's experience with this disease, the disease can be controlled to the point where the person can lead a productive life. There can be long periods where the patient has normal mood swings that we all have. If the person does experience an exaggerated mood swing, he or she and his or her doctor can take steps to control this exaggerated mood swing appropriately and quickly. After this control the patient can return to what can be a normal life.

Here again, I must emphasize the patient must have continual follow-up with their doctor or medical professional. As with other diseases, treatment of this condition requires close monitoring by a professional person who is an expert in treating the disease. The patient (and those close to him or her) also should have a thorough knowledge of how the disease acts.

I previously mentioned that a very important aspect of controlling this disease is the fact the patient should be adept at "<u>listening to his or her body</u>" and realize when they are getting off center with regard to their emotional state. My doctors taught me how to do this and it helped me to recognize when an emotional swing could be impending. Once they had pointed this out me I could feel myself starting up or down. You can feel the up and down feelings even when they are less than major.

Personal relationships with spouses, family members, friends, co-workers and others can be adversely affected by patients with this disease. Lifelong relationships can be damaged or lost. This is one of the most tragic consequences of bipolar disorder.

My wife and I were fortunate enough to have two wonderful children. The both are successful professionals as adults. Apparently, my bipolar disorder did not have any significant negative long-term effects on them.

Later in my life I developed kidney failure as a complication of lithium therapy. My daughter donated one of her kidneys to me. This is another example of the grace of God being present in my life. I am forever grateful to her for giving me this gift of life.

As with all diseases, the patient with bipolar disorder or any mental illness can benefit from a good support group around them. This group can consist of family, friends and others with this disease. Specific disease support groups can provide a good source of knowledge for the patient and show the patient that they are not the only ones struggling with their disease.

In my case, my wife wanted nothing to do with my problems. We were majorly incompatible in many ways and this was an indication of that. This may have been fortunate for me. I was used to getting out adverse situations by myself.

I did spend a year or so in a diversion program for doctors who had experienced a substance abuse problem. Although substance abuse was not my problem, I did share my experiences with them. This program was very beneficial for me and definitely functioned as a support group for me.

In my experience in the world of sports, I quickly became aware of the fact that players continued to play the game even though they have an injury. I have seen this many times during my athletic career. I have admired those who continued to play in the game despite their injury.

This playing with an injury occurs in every facet of life we all experience. There is someone we know who is continuing to live their lives as best they can even though they have a physical or mental limitation in their life.

My greatest admiration is for those who continue to play in the game of life even though they have a physical, mental or developmental disability. It touches my heart to see these people going on with their lives even though they are dealing with such disabilities. When I see a person with no legs pushing themselves along on a skate board I think my injury is minimal compared to theirs. When I see a Down's syndrome person working hard at their job, I get the same feeling. When I see a mentally ill person trying to compensate for their disability, I feel the same.

When I see our medical school class president, Dr. Tony Sebastian, continue his distinguished career (Professor of Nephrology at UCSF Medical School) even though he has a progressive neurologic disease that has placed him in a hospital bed with continuous respiratory support by way of a tracheostomy, I have unsurpassed admiration for him. I am honored to be his friend. My classmates feel the same. We are a very close group.

And I am supposed to complain because I have bipolar disorder? I don't think so!

There are many examples of these types of people in our world today. I have a great deal of empathy, respect and admiration for them. One person once said to me, "you're always for the underdog, aren't you?" I'm not sure how she concluded that, but I saw it as a great compliment for any person.

I would like to bring up another point again. As we know, this disease is congenital and the patient will have the disease from birth. In the years before the diagnosis of this disease is made the patient could have sub-clinical manifestations of its presence in them. These manifestations could fly below the radar and not be significant enough to result in the diagnosis of this disease in the person. This person might exhibit great enthusiasm for what they were doing and they might perform better than they ordinarily would. Could this be a benefit from having this disease? What do you think?

Such an example may explain why some people became successful in business or other fields, before and after the diagnosis of bipolar disorder was made in their life. I have asked myself if I thought that my focused enthusiasm for learning about medicine and practicing it the way I did was possibly a positive by-product of having bipolar disorder.

One attitude I developed during my years as a doctor in California was that I felt a sense of responsibility to all the patients in California. I had been educated in California and the people there had helped me to learn medicine. I had no problem to help in any way to assist those caring for the patient (go get blood, move a table, push a respirator, start an IV, wipe the floor, etc.). Also, I had no problem in throwing in my two cents if I thought I could be helpful in caring for the patient. Occasionally that got me into some trouble.

During my lifetime, I have been exposed to many unique situations and coincidental situations. Don't ask me why I was exposed to so many unique and unusual events. Perhaps it was because I was a curious person who was involved in many diverse activities during my life. I'm going to share with you some of these unusual experiences I have had in the second part of the book.

After coming from Niagara Falls New York as a one year old (my parents were from Canada), I grew up in the mountains of W.Va., outside the city of Charleston. Charleston is located on the Kanawha River in the south-central part of the state. The city is surrounded by the Appalachian Mountains.

You will meet the subsistence farmers far back into the mountains of W. Va. These people are descendants of the original settlers of the state. They chose to maintain their simple isolated life rather than join the rest of society in its progression.

You will learn of the exceptional athletes that came out of the Kanawha Valley during that time. Many of my friends attended major colleges and universities on athletic scholarships. Some of them played their way out of the potential of a lifetime of work in the coal mines or in the steel mills of W.Va. and Pennsylvania. Some were able to play their way into professional sports.

I met the great heavyweight champion boxer, Jack Dempsey in Jessie Ferris's barbershop when I was about six years old. Jessie was a boxing promoter in Charleston.

I will be able to describe to you the atmosphere in southwest Los Angeles County in the late 50's. These were the days were depicted in the movies: "Happy Days", "Rebel Without a Cause" and "Blackboard Jungle". They were the days of Elvis Presley, Buddy Holly, Fats Domino, Little Richard, and other great singers. I finished high school in Torrance, California. I will tell you of my experience with Louis Zamperini while there.

I will tell you of my many experiences at UCLA. These experiences occurred in the classrooms and in the UCLA football program. We worked with and played against many well-known coaches and players in the football program.

During this part of the book I will explain in detail some of the physiologic problems one can have with vigorous exercise in hot weather.

Some of the most unusual events occurred while I was in the Greek fraternity system at UCLA. You will hear of funny to hilarious events I encountered in this area.

You will meet the wonderful students of my medical school class at the University of California Medical School in San Francisco, California. It's a wonder that we got through that great medical school considering how much fun we had there. There's no way you could envision the hilarious situations we found ourselves in during our four years there.

Our professors felt we were way ahead of our time in being able to manufacture fun for ourselves during those very rigorous years of learning. My wife and I were married during my third year in medical school. We were in love, but that marriage, even though it lasted 31 years and produced two wonderful children, was anything but traditional.

The next adventure I will share with you is my one year internship at Los Angeles County (the "Big County") Hospital. The Watts Riot of 1965 happened one month after we got there as interns. You will learn of the medical treatment of the injured rioters and first responders during that riot. I will share with you my experiences while taking house calls in Los Angeles after my internship.

I'm going to tell you of my experiences in the war in Vietnam during the late 60's. I will share some parts of that war with you, including the photos the US Navy corpsman and I took during the year we were there. Along with other significant events that occurred in Vietnam when we were there, was the 1968 Tet Offensive. I will tell you of my unique experience on the day that Tet Offensive began.

Later in the book you will learn of the state of kidney transplants in the 1970's. As a urology resident at the University of Oregon Medical School Hospital I was intimately involved with the kidney transplant program.

After finishing the urology residency, I joined two excellent urologists in a practice in Southern California. My private practice started very well. Three years after I started practice I had my first severe depression. I nearly lost my life at that time.

Five years after that first major depression I was diagnosed as having bipolar disorder. I will share how bipolar disorder affected me from the time of diagnosis to the present time.

Also, during this part of the book I will tell you of some of the unique situations I ran into while practicing urology. You will find these situations to be interesting, informative and, at times, quite humorous.

Before I go on to the reminder of this book I would like to tell you of the tremendous honors I have received during my interesting life. These unappalled honors I have received include: 1) The honor to have had wonderful parents and sister. What I learned from them never left me throughout my life. I am proud of my Canadian families. 2) The honor I had to be in my own family. My wife and I were married in San Francisco and had our daughter there while l was in medical school. Our son was born 4 years later when I was in Vietnam. 3) The honor to have spent time with my wonderful friends in Charleston, W.Va. and Torrance, California. 4) The honor to attend UCSF Medical School in San Francisco. 5) The honor to participate as a doctor in the Vietnam War, where I could help the American and allied soldiers and the Vietnamese people. 6) The honor to learn Urology under the guidance of Clarence V. Hodges, MD, who was a Noble Prize winner in medicine. 7) The honor to hear from a fellow general surgery resident that he had learned more from me about patient care than he had from any other doctor he had known, including his professors (This was a testimony to the exceptional people I learned medicine from). 8) The honor to hear the gratitude expressed by my patients for helping them.

If you wish to see the part of my life when I developed obvious signs and symptoms of bipolar disorder go to the chapter or section entitled Private Practice.

The previous chapters or sections of the book describe the many unique experiences I had prior to the diagnosis of bipolar disorder. During the time of those experiences, I may have been manifesting subliminal expressions of bipolar disorder. I believe you will find these chapters or sections of the book interesting and informative.

Chapter 2

A Life With Bipolar Disorder

Things began rather routinely for me. My sister and I were born in Niagara Falls, New York. She was born in 1938 and I was born in 1939. Our mother was born and grew up in the small Canadian town of Burks Falls, Ontario. Our father was born and grew up in Niagara Falls, Canada. They met and married in Niagara Falls, Canada. My sister and I were born in Niagara Falls, NY. We were blessed to have wonderful parents. They were always there when we needed them and they took a great interest in our lives. I am proud of my Canadian heritage.

During the depression of the 30's my father witnessed the dare devils at that time trying to earn money at Niagara Falls by doing death defying stunts at the falls. These stunts included going over the falls in various types of contraptions. Some even lived!

Tight rope walking was very popular at the falls. One guy took a table and chair out there and ate his lunch high above the falls.

The Second World War would begin in 1939 when the Germans invaded Poland. Our father worked in an essential wartime industry. In 1940 he was transferred from the plant in Niagara Falls to the large Union Carbide plant in South Charleston, West Virginia, which was a few miles south of Charleston. As you know, our involvement in WWII began in December 1941.

Charleston is the capital city of West Virginia and is located on the Kanawha River in southern West Virginia. It is surrounded by the Appalachian Mountains. These mountains have a great deal to do with the history and development of this part of the state. The mountains are not especially high, when compared to other mountains in our country, but their sides are very steep and they are densely packed with trees and foliage. These topographical features made travel through the mountains very difficult for the Indians and early settlers of our country, thus many of the settlements and eventual cities of West Virginia are located on rivers.

Daniel Boone lived here for a time before he moved west into Kentucky. He mapped out the Cumberland Gap and trail. This trail through the Application Mountains allowed settlers to travel into Kentucky easily, when compared to a trip through these rough mountains between the Kanawha valley and Kentucky. There are many sites around Charleston that commemorate Daniel Boone. One of my junior high school teachers apparently was a descendent of his.

During the Civil War, large military units could not travel by land through these rugged mountains. Small units of the Northern and Southern armies traveled by way of the rivers or river valleys. Most or the battles of the Civil War in this area of West Virginia were a form of guerrilla warfare consisting of ambush type fighting between small units along the rivers and adjacent mountains. They often pitted family against family.

After the war some of these battles continued as skirmishes, or small battles, between groups of people or even different families. Such conflicts are thought to be the origin of the famous "family feuds" (i.e., Hatfield's and Mc Coy's) that occurred in the mountains of the southeastern United States after the Civil War. The two families lived on the opposite's sides the Ohio River near what today is Huntington, West Virginia. A small incident (i.e. loss of a hog) ignited a long-standing war between these two families. This war even accounted for some deaths in these families.

I think it would be interesting to take a moment to look at the medical care available to those Civil War soldiers during that war. From the point of view of medicine at that time, the ability to kill soldiers was much more advanced than the ability to treat wounded or diseased soldiers. The breach loading rifles used by the Union Army used a mini-ball ammunition and the barrels of their guns were rifled (circular groves in the barrels of the rifles) that induced spin to the mini-ball making this firearm very accurate. The spinning of a bullet makes it fly much straighter. The mini-ball was also of a very large caliber round and could produce devastating injury to the soldier (interestingly, this round does not produce the amount of damage that the modern high speed smaller round which tumbles when it penetrates the body). The breach loading rifle that was simpler and quicker to load than the mussel loading rifle being used by southern Confederate troops and, thus, the Union soldier could fire his rifle at a more rapid rate than the rebel soldier could using a mussel loading rifle with a slower method of loading. This meant that the Union soldiers had a greater fire power than their counterparts in the Confederate army.

The Confederate soldiers, as a group, were much better shots than the Union soldiers. This fact never made up for the fact that the Union soldiers had more firepower. Later in the war some Union troops were using the first lever action repeating rifle (the Spencer repeating rifle), making their fire power even greater than it was with their breach loading rifles and could be as much as ten times as great as the Confederate firepower.

Accurate artillery cannons were used on both sides and produced devastating wounds to soldiers on both sides. Hand to hand fighting could involve the use of bayonets and knives furthering the severity of wounds of the soldiers of both sides.

There was basically no ambulance services available in the early part of the war. Early in the war a simple buggy was used as an ambulance to carry wounded soldiers off the battlefield. Other soldiers were carried of the battlefield by their comrades. Those soldiers who could walk would try to walk to a primitive hospital. These hospitals frequently were confiscated local houses which were crudely converted into hospitals.

These grossly inefficient means of transporting and slow ways of moving a wounded soldier off the battlefield meant that wounded soldiers could lie where the fell for long periods of times, even up to days or weeks. Because of these circumstances, soldiers could die on the field of battle from bleeding (even in the cases of the simplest bleeding from a minor wounds) and most certainly wound infections and resultant septicemia.

When or if these soldiers got to a primitive field hospital their chance of survival was bleak. There were no antibiotics to treat infection. Anesthesia was also primitive and many of the soldiers had surgery without anaesthesia.

Dr. Letterman of the Union Army devised and implemented the first ambulance corps of the United States Army. This was used first in the battle at Antietam and greatly improved the survival of the Union soldiers. This corps has been a vital part of the medical care of American soldiers since that time. The

U.S. Army Letterman Hospital is located at the Presidio in San Francisco. Some of my medical school classmates trained in this hospital.

One interesting fact was the fact a soldier could survive a through and through chest wound if the wound did not involve any vital organ (heart) or any major vessels of the lung. Wounds to the abdomen were universally fatal. If the soldier did not die right away from internal bleeding, he would die from an overwhelming infection that occurred with these types of wounds. This fact may have given rise to the term "gut shot". Surgeons would come around and stick their finger into the wound and move their finger around to allow the infection to drain. This maneuver had no chance of improving survival and may have worsened the survival of the patient.

The only real chance of the wounded soldier to survive was that if he was wounded in one of his extremities (arms or legs) and that extremity was removed either totally, or in part, because of tissue destruction, gangrene or bleeding. This surgery was done by doctors practicing no form of sterile technique. As I said, anesthesia was poor or nonexistent. They simply used a saw and a primitive type of suture to tie blood vessels off with. This surgery may have been the origin of the term "saw bones". I must point out to you that an extremity amputation is not an easy operation. Many soldiers died during these surgeries. Surgery was not a very well-developed part of medicine at that time. Removed extremities were piled up outside these primitive operating tents.

This explains the fact that the surviving wounded veterans of the Civil War usually have a part of their extremities removed. They are seen in photographs with part or all of one to four of their extremities removed.

General Stonewall Jackson, who was from a part of Virginia that would become part of the new state of West Virginia after the war, died from pneumonia which developed after part of his left arm was removed. He was shot in his arm by friendly fire from a Confederate sentry soldier. You can visit the site of his death in northern Virginia. He died in a guest house on the plantation home of a friend of his. He is revered in the state of West Virginia and there are many schools and parks named for him in the Charleston area where I grew up.

One thing that is not mentioned often is the fact that as many of the soldiers survived as did is a reflection that they were usually healthy young people and had very strong immune systems. Unfortunately, when these young men were placed into prisoner of war camps and starved their immune systems deteriorated and they were susceptible to many diseases that they may have otherwise survived if they had not been starved.

Many of the types of wounds seen in this war would be easily and successfully be treated with our advanced knowledge and techniques of treatment of war wounds that we have today. In addition to the loss of life from war wounds there were infectious diseases such as cholera and infectious dysentery that could take your life.

There was no medical care available in the POW camps. The death rate in these camps was very high. Because of these conditions the loss of American lives was devastatingly high. It is often pointed out that there were more American lives were lost in this war than in other war in our history. This fact was because of the high mortality rate from war wounds, the very poor hospital facilities, primitive surgery, starvation in the prisoner of war camps and the overwhelming presence of severe and fatal infectious diseases in these camps.

There was a foundation of a previous Civil War fort not far from where we lived in the low mountains east of the city. The fort must have changed hands many times during the war. A sign there mentions the South's shelling of a Northern garrison along the river from this fort in 1862. We spent many days playing in and around this fort foundation.

Little did I know, when I was growing up in and around those Civil War battlefields in West Virginia, that years later I would be involved, as a doctor, in a war which was characterized by the same small unit, ambush guerrilla type of fighting in Vietnam.

The beautiful rugged mountains West Virginia are also the home of "Bluegrass" music and the famous "white lighting" alcohol stills. Both of these entities can still be found in these mountains today. In addition to "white lighting", a new commodity in recent years has appeared in the mountains of Appalachia. Ginseng is a very valuable herb used in the orient for seasoning and as a possible aphrodisiac. Most of the ginseng from these mountains ends up in Asia after it goes through a series of "brokers" from the pickers to its eventual destination in Asia. It is a very valuable product on the foreign market.

This plant is now grown by some of the people in the Appalachian Mountains known as ginseng farmers. In some cases local people will grow the ginseng on their land or in specific plots they have chosen.

Here's where things get a little dicey. These growers defend their plots of ginseng plants fiercely. It takes a few years for the ginseng plant to mature to a point where it can be harvested. During this plant's maturing time and during harvest time it is not uncommon for other diggers to try to steal these plants. The owners commonly have dogs and use weapons (guns, etc.) to defend their plots. Here is where one-way or two-way gunshot exchanges can occur. This is not dissimilar to some of the fighting in the Civil War seen in these areas.

A friend of mine was a distinguished surgeon in San Diego, California. His first job after WW11 was as a general practioner back in the mountains of West Virginia. One night he had to climb under a bridge to get away from a gunfight in the town. This issue was not insignificant in his decision to leave that job and do a residency in general surgery.

If you add into the equation, the illegal growth of marijuana by some people back in the mountains, things can start to look like the "old wild west", especially when the state and federal agencies get involved in trying to stop the illegal growing of this plant. In contrast to this "wild west" flavor in the backcountry mountains of the state, the modern cities of the state are more sophisticated and very conscious of the environment. The state today is a favorite destination for those seeking the beauty and recreation adventures found in the state.

In 1940, Charleston was a bustling industrial city like Pittsburg, Pa. and the steel town of Wheeling, W.Va. Union Carbide's largest plant in the country was located along the river in South Charleston. DuPont had a very large plant not far away. Chemicals were being produced by both plants. These chemicals were transported north by railroad tank cars. There were other industrial plants located along the river. The waste materials produced by these plants were dumped into the Kanawha River as it coursed thru the Kanawha valley.

The coal industry was huge in southern West Virginia during those years and was an integral part of the state's economy. Coal was constantly being transported north by train to the steel mills of northern West Virginia and Pennsylvania. It was also transported by river barges. The many sounds of coal burning trains went on day and night. Natural gas was a big product of the state.

Pollution of the air and the rivers was a fact of life. The air was polluted by the smoke from the coal burning trains, smoke from the chemical plants and smoke from coal burning furnaces we all used for heating. The Kanawha river, which coursed through the city, was heavily contaminated by the waste material from the large plants.

Some tributaries of the river were contaminated with coal dust as they flowed through the coal country. I learned to swim in the Coal River. This river was completely black having passed through the coal fields. If you went under the surface of this river you could not see anything but pure black water. We did not open our eyes underwater. Your bathing suit or any other clothing that got wet was impregnated with coal dust. Despite all these minor inconveniences it was still great to swim in this river.

If you had a white house it would turn grey in two or three years. We seemed always to be painting our house. Much of the home heating was provided by coal burning furnaces in many parts of the city. These family homes had a coal bin in the basement. This heating system added to the already polluted air. The funny thing is that nobody talked about pollution. We thought it was a normal part of life in a bustling and dynamic industrial city.

Because Charleston was the capital of West Virginia, there were plenty of state and national politics to go around. The state was a long-time democratic stronghold. It was the second stop, after New Hampshire, in the democratic primaries.

A year after we arrived in Charleston we moved to the top of one of the low mountains east of the Kanawha River. There were four houses in this small neighborhood and the road ended just past our house. Beyond that point where the forests of West Virginia. Because of the restriction of building supplies and construction during WW11, the neighborhood would remain the same until well after the war.

As a child I was outdoor oriented and very shy. My pre-school years were spent running and the woods around our neighborhood, playing games and collecting small animals. My sister collected turtles. I basically spent long hours in the forest with my dog. We were always on the lookout for snakes in the area.

Occasionally, we could be very responsible kids and took every opportunity to preform our civic duties (I'm being a little generous in describing our motivation to do this.). For example, we tried to help keep our neighborhoods clean. In our part of the mountains on warm summer nights lovers liked to park in a local rock quarry at the bottom of our hill. We actually were fairly liberal on the issue of the personal rights of people parking and making love in their car, but, at the same time, we objected to them leaving their various love-making paraphernalia lying all over the ground. I'm talking a lot of condoms and an occasional pair of lady's panties. We felt it was our civic duty (Again, a little generous as to our motivation.) to try to get rid of the problem. We came up with a simple and unique solution for this problem.

We would hide in the woods at night and throw buckeyes or dirt clods down on the cars of these lovers. We were hopeful to hit the top of their car or trunk of their car while they were in a heated love lock inside the car.

We got good at it. Those buckeyes or dirt clods would hit the cars with a high level of consistency. Man, some of those guys got real mad. They would jump out of their cars pulling up their pants while cursing at us loudly. What could they do? It was dark, we were well hidden, and we knew those woods like the back of our hands. If they started out after us, they were the ones who would get lost in the dark. After all our efforts at this civic duty, the love-making traffic in the quarry did slow down significantly. We felt we had done our part in trying to preserve the natural beauty of our state.

I took up driving very early. I was 7 or 8 when I got started in earnest. My next-door neighbor was nice enough to let me sit on his lap and steer the car along while he was driving. Forget the fact that I had not considered extensively how to stop the car. Also the hill was steep as it coursed down the mountain. One evening I got into his car, took the brake off, coasted back onto the street, turned left and started my adventure down the mountain.

The neighbor across the street was eating dinner when he saw this car go by with the top of a small head in the driver's window. He jumped up, ran out of his house, ran across his lawn, jumped the hedge and reached the car in time to jump in on the left side and stop the car. I wasn't really the hero of the neighborhood after I tried to drive that car down the hill. I'm s sure some of the adults in the neighborhood got a bigger laugh out of it than my parents did. Can you imagine what would have happened to me if our hero good samaritan neighbor (Mr. Scott) had already finished his dinner when I went driving by in that '48 Ford.

We went to grade school in a two-room school down the hill from the Civil War fort foundation. Actually, there were five rooms in the school. There were two classrooms, two bathrooms and a cloak room (where we put our coats and lunches). Grades one to three were taught in one classroom and grades four to six were taught in the second classroom. You were asked to put your head down on your desk while the other grades were being taught in your room. As you can guess, some of the smarter kids listened when they had their heads on their desks and got the jump on the rest of us for the next grade. I didn't like them very much.

In West Virginia, at that time, you did not advance on to the next grade until you passed the grade you were in. A teenager might be in the third grade with you. This happened in our school. An older boy (thirteen years old) from Tanner Hollow was in the fourth grade with us. In West Virginia the hollows are located between the hills and some of them were named. Another hollow across the river was called Magazine Hollow. This guy from Tanner Hollow was a big and very rough person.

One day he ambushed my sister and I as we were walking home from school. We had cut through the woods and he ambushed us there. He intimated me and tied my sister to a tree. Finally, a neighbor saw us from the road and helped to untie my sister. We basically stayed out of his way after that. My friend and I were later ambushed by three guys from Magazine Hollow. I will tell you about that soon.

The two teachers in our grade school had their choice of disciplinary actions they could administer depending on the severity of the offence we committed. For lighter offences, you might have to write on the chalk board the specific offence you had committed many times. For the next level of offence, you might have to stand alone in the cloak room for varying periods of time, again depending on the relative severity of the offence. By far the worst and most embarrassing discipline was to be taken to the cloak room where you would have to pull your pants down and then be paddled by your teacher. To avoid further embarrassment, I always tried to make sure I was wearing clean underwear. You never knew when you would be revealing your underwear.

Speaking of underwear, I went to my first Carbide summer camp for the children of Carbide employees when I was about six years old. My mother told me to change my underwear every day. I was very shy and was not going to change my underwear in front of other people, especially not every day. I solved the problem by putting on a new pair of underwear every day over the ones I already had on. I had some difficulty explaining why I had seven pair of underwear on when my parents picked me up 1 week later. Obviously, I had been swimming every day in my fashionable multi-underwear suit. As I said, I was a very shy child.

Things got a little tough with the underwear situation while I was at this summer camp. We were learning to swim in the "Coal River". This river can through the coal mines and was completely black in color. By the end of the week I had seven pair of damp underwear on and they were various shades of grey depend ending of how much of coal dust was impregnated in them. I was very glad to get home where I could extricate myself from that plaster-like cast of damp, grey underwear I had created for myself.

Little League baseball started around 1951. I met many lifelong friends among those Little League players. It was here where I sustained a significant concussion while sliding into third base. There were many interesting athletic activities and events around the Kanawha Valley during those years. I was beginning to find an identity for myself as a student athlete.

There was a barber in Charleston who was also a professional boxing promoter in the city. I was about 6 yrs. old my dad took me into his (Jessie Ferris) barber shop for a haircut. He asked if I would like to meet Jack Dempsey. There was a dark-haired man sitting in a corner chair. I went over and shook his hand. He asked me if that was my dad over there. I turned my head to see who he was pointing to and said, "Yes". When I turned my head back my face ran into his large clenched fist. He told me to never make that mistake again. This was in 1946 or 1947 and Jack Dempsey would have been 50-60 yrs. old or so.

Charleston had a triple A (AAA) professional baseball team in the American Association named the Charleston Senators. As part of the "knot hole" club as kids we frequently went to the games at the ball park. There were teams from Minneapolis, Indianapolis and other cities in the league. They were farm teams of the major league teams.

There are those who think Willie Mays never played in the minor leagues. They say he went right to the major leagues without playing in the minors. I hate to tell them that we saw Willie Mays playing for the Minneapolis Millers in Charleston one night. He did play a few games with the Millers before going on to the New York Giants. Oh yea, Herb Score was pitching for Indianapolis that night.

We played sand-lot baseball and football in those grade school years. Our five-man football team played a team from another neighborhood from the next mountain north of us. We had a very sophisticated and deceptive offense. We had had one fold-up helmet and whoever ran the ball got to wear it.

I had superb physical trainers when I was growing up. Today you would pay a lot of money to have access to the physical trainers I had. My trainers were my dad and our neighbors. My dad had me dig up a large part of our back yard for a garden. The West Virginia red clay is very hard to dig up. I spent many hours digging up that clay and preparing it for a garden. You talk about cross training, that was it! My dad and several our neighbors allowed me cut and trim their yards for money. I used the old fashion push mowers and trimmed the yards with a hand operated trimmer. Using this trimmer with my right and left hand, I spent hours trimming these lawns. I developed strong hands and forearms. They have machines in gyms now that have you develop strength in your hands and forearms.

I delivered newspapers on my heavy one speed bike through the mountains. I carried the load of papers on the front of my bike. This was a total body work-out. I developed balanced strength between my arms, legs and trunk. This work-out was like an orangutan swinging through the trees of the jungle.

They don't have time to stop and decide which muscle group they're working on. The orangutan is not "buffed up" with big muscles, but is extremely strong.

Speaking of orangutans, there was a guy who barn stormed the country with an orangutan in the 1930's. He set up a boxing ring and took entry fees. He would pay anyone a large prize if they could stay in the ring with this muzzled orangutan for one minute. Within seconds the orangutan would have an over 200 lb. man cowering and shaking in a corner of the ring with most of his cloths torn off.

This type of well-balanced strength helped me in baseball and football. Later in my life this type of strength was a great asset in doing surgery. In surgery, I could retract (pull aside) organs and large amounts tissue with my hands and forearms for long periods of time (much longer than my colleagues).

Local hollows around the city were referred to as "hollers". Some of the boys from these hollers were very rough and very intimidating to us. I already mentioned the incident where one of the holler boys attacked my sister and I when we were in grade school. When I was in junior high school, my friend and I were walking back home from a pool party one night when we were attacked by three boys from Magazine Hollow (on the other side of the city). A car drove past us and blue flames came out of it's dual exhausts as it backfired loudly. Three of them got out of their car and began to follow us down this dark road. I think they hit me first because I was the bigger of the two of us. I landed at the base of a wall next to the road. My friend took off running. I got up and was looking at three, less than congenial looking, guys standing there. By that time, I had played a lot of football. They did not look nearly as tough as the players I played against every day. I ran hard through them and was able to knock one of them down while my friend got away.

Then I ran like hell. I outran the three boys for quite a distance. Finally, I was getting tired and decided to stop in this open garage in the neighborhood to rest. I heard this labored breathing coming from somewhere in that dark garage. Unbelievably, it was coming from my friend. He had stopped in the same garage to rest!!! I mean there were a lot houses in that community. How in the world did we end up in the same garage? My friend took off and ran all the way to his house. I called my dad from a house in the neighborhood and he came to get me.

West Virginia became a state after the Civil War and was considered to be a border state. The city of Charleston could be considered a northern or southern city (your choice) in the late 40's and 50's. There seemed to be different socioeconomic levels (or strata) of the society in the city. At the top were the professionals (bankers, doctors, lawyers, and dentists), politicians and owners of large businesses. The white-collar workers were at the second level. These included engineers, executive and junior executives in companies and other white-collar workers. The next level down were the blue-collar workers. Because of the huge numbers of industrial industries (coal, chemicals, glass, etc.) in the city, this group was the largest group of people in the city. The coal industry was the biggest industry in the state. The people working in the coal industry lived near the coal mines in cities outside the urban cities. Railroad companies were critical for the transportation of industrial products. My dad was a foreman at the Union Carbide plant. Thousands of the men and women worked in these industries. The next level down were the service industries of house keepers, newspaper salesmen and street maintenance workers act.

Beyond these groups were a group of subsistence farmers who lived deep in the woods. They lived an isolated life and seemed to have no interest in participating in the contemporary society. They were believed to be descendants of the original settlers of the state. They spoke a type of dialect of English not spoken by others in the state. I met them when I was working at a Carbide summer camp. The camp was also located deep into the woods. You reached the camp by riding a single car two-way train to the end of the tracks. After that, you walked a couple of miles to reach the camp.

One day, while we were working in the camp craft shop, a young boy came walking out of the woods. He was bare footed. He had walked through the forest full of snakes without shoes on. We gave him a Robin Hood hat that the campers had made in the craft shop.

He quickly ran back into the woods. The next day he returned with his older brother. We gave him a hat also. We asked them where they lived. They pointed toward the woods. We asked if they could show us where they lived.

We walked for a couple of miles into the woods and came to a small village. There were 6 or 7 houses in the village. There were horses and cows in a corral. There were gardens between the houses. The houses were crudely constructed and the windows had shutters, but some had no glass in them. We saw some horse drawn farm equipment and a couple of old pickup trucks. The adults were indifferent towards us. They made no attempt to interact with us.

These people were true subsistence farmers. They were very isolated and weren't interested in interacting with other people. They may have been some of the "Blue Grass" singers in our country. They had wonderful singers and exceptional instrumentalists among them. These people played and sang some of the original folk music in America. They were scattered through the Appalachian Mountains of the south central part of our country. The boys we met said they had dropped out of school after the third grade. I did not know how, or if, these people were able to make the money they needed to buy the small amount of goods they needed to augment their subsistence foods they provided for themselves.

We had to go into the city for Jr. High School. The academic instruction in our junior high school was excellent. There seemed to be an extra-curricular activity for most of the kids. There was the band and many types of clubs. My friends and I focused on athletics. In those days, we all wanted to play multiple sports. We played football, baseball, basketball and track.

Our junior high school team.
(grades 7th, 8th, 9th)

Initially, I was not anxious to play football. I finally decided to play after two tough players came up to me and told me that if I did not play they were going to have to do a little blocking and tackling on the side. Their attitude convinced me that playing was the better of the two options they presented to me. Little did I know at that time that I would end my football career playing for UCLA in Los Angeles, California.

In football, we did run into a few problems. There was that same old problem of older people being in your grade level. I remember when I was in the ninth grade we were playing football against a junior high school in Dunbar, West

Virginia. Some guy hit me and I lost half of one of my front teeth (it had been capped earlier). That guy had a dark beard and was bigger than the rest of us. I thought he worked in the mines and was playing for the local junior high school football team on the side.

Another problem was that some of the junior high school players chewed tobacco while they were playing. Man, the game was hard enough as it was without some dude spitting tobacco juice at you. Six or seven players from our junior high team went to large colleges on football scholarships. One ended up playing for the New York Giants. The leagues were very well organized for the six junior high schools in the city.

For us, Charleston High School was a big step up. The academics were more intense. There were many more academic and social clubs for the students. Industrial arts was a big department. Our band traveled to some national events to play. There were fraternities and sororities at the school. I was lucky to be able to play football and baseball there. It's hard to describe the number of wonderful people at that high school. I'm so fortunate to have been around them. Elvis Presley made his national debut when I was a junior in that high school.

Our American Legion baseball team played all over the state. In some of the small cities we played in it wasn't unusual for there to be a set of "local rules". I remember once we were playing a game in Clay, West Virginia. We were well ahead in the fourth inning, when the umpire suspended the game. He said he couldn't be late to start the evening shift at a local mine.

High school football in Charleston and around the state was very highly developed, similar to what we might see in the state of Texas today. Although we did not redshirt (skip a year of playing football to extend your high school eligibility) high school players, families were moved to the city in order for their sons to play for a city team. Our cross-town rival high school did move a family to Charleston so their son could play football for their team.

Of the 60 players on our high school team, 15-18 players or more went to prestigious universities around the country on football scholarships. One of our players went on to play professional football. Many went on to become productive professionals later in their life.

One of the basketball players not far from where we went to school was a great player. He was a great college, Olympic and professional basketball player. He was inducted into the college and professional hall of fame and he is on the logo on the NBA basketball today. I've never met him, but I would go to games where he was playing against our high school. His name is Jerry West. He also played with and against my friends in the summer league in Charleston.

Later in my life an unbelievable coincidence occurred. A medical school classmate of mine, Earl Shultz, played basketball at the University of California and played against Jerry West and West Virginia University in the national championship series. Earl and Jerry became lifelong friends and played in the Olympics together. Earl became a radiologist and Jerry went on to make more history in the NBA and beyond. Another striking coincident was that Earl actually lived along the Kanawha River in Charleston when he was young.

Four of my friends at Charleston High School were very good basketball players. They all went to Virginia Tech (known as VPI then) and started for the basketball team as freshmen. One of them, Chris Smith, made All American at Virginia Tech. He became the CEO of the Union Carbide plant in Charleston. He was recently inducted into the West Virginia Hall of Fame. My good friend, Dean Blake, was one of the four players. He also pitched for the VPI baseball team. He became an excellent civil engineer. Jerry Smith played in Colorado.

It could be boring for us at times around the city of Charleston. Occasionally we had to take some risks to find entertainment. I will tell you only one of the many events we created for ourselves in those years.

There was an annual festive river boat race in Charleston. The race was between two large river boats pushing a single barge up the river. It was the highlight of a summer "River Festival". Before the race started my friend, Bill Green, and I jumped off a bridge unto one of the barges that was being pushed by one of the boats in the race. We walked down the barge to the river boat and joined the people on the boat. We were actually like two stowaways who had snuck onto the boat for this exciting race. We had a great time on our boat including having to go for food and drinks for some of the distinguished people on the boat. My friend actually helped serve some state politicians on our boat during the race.

The adventures we had in the mountains and around the city of Charleston are too numerous to point out here. Suffice it to say it seemed that there was never a dull moment in our young lives. An airport was built near Charleston in the mid 50's. They made it by shaving off the tops of two mountains. It has short runways and to this day commercial jets cannot land there. If you are flying to Charleston, you might have to transfer to a smaller propeller plane in an adjoining state.

In the fall of 1955 our dad told us he had been transferred to the Carbide plant in Torrance, California. In February 1956, we went to Los Angeles, California.

It was such a pleasure for me to grow up with this wonderful group of young women and men of our city. I cannot tell you of all the most wonderful people that lived and worked in and around Charleston. I know there were many wonderful places to grow up in our country during those years. For me, I could not have wished for a better place to be. Perhaps my dad was right when he told me many years later," You could take the boy out of the country, but you cannot take the country out of the boy"

Chapter 3

The Beach Cities of Southwest Los Angeles County

My mother, my sister and I flew to Los Angeles in February of 1956. My dad was already there working at the Union Carbide plant in Torrance, California. As we landed in Los Angeles I could not believe there was a city as large as that in the world. The city went on for miles and miles.

My dad bought a house in a nice neighborhood. We lived on the edge of Redondo Beach, California, and my sister and I attended Torrance high school. When we arrived there and started school in the middle of the school year, it was a bit of a cultural shock to us. We had come from an extremely traditional mid-Atlantic industrial city. In California things were much more progressive and casual. Culturally, it seemed like we had walked onto the set of the movie of "Blackboard Jungle".

The first thing I noticed was the fact that people were wearing "floppies", or what I thought were shower shoes, to school. That's definitely not the preferred shoe to wear in West Virginia with all those snakes slithering around. The styles of dress were much more casual. Beyond that that there were many of the features of the "Happy Days of the 50's". Many of the cars were modified into cool hotrods. Car clubs were plentiful.

Because I played football and baseball I quickly made friends in the athletic department. I quickly discovered that there were many great people among the students of our school. I have many lifelong friends from Torrance High School. It's just that the atmosphere in and around Los Angeles was a little different than it was in the city along the banks of the Kanawha River in southern West Virginia.

The beach cities of Redondo Beach, Hermosa Beach and Manhattan Beach were beautiful. These cities would become among the most exclusive real estate in the Los Angeles area. We spent our high school leisure time lounging, body surfing and playing volleyball at these beach cities. The kids were surfing with long boards. Some of them were making these boards in the garages of the small houses along the beach. They would carve the boards out of balsa wood, sand them down, apply a resin cloth and then epoxy on them. Many of the boards were decorated beautifully.

The major beaches south of Torrance were Long Beach, Huntington Beach, Laguna Beach, San Clemente and San 'Onophre, which was south of San Clemente and just inside the large Marine Corps base, Camp Pendleton. The Laguna

Beach greeter was seen every day in that city. Between these major surfing sites there were large stretches of deserted beaches. One stretch was called "Tin Can Beach" because people left their used tin cans on the beach. A surfer in college at UCLA was making surfing movies He made surfing movies that were documentaries on the surfing life. They were studded with humor and were priceless to those who watched them.

People were riding skate boards made of two by fours with metal skates nailed to each end of the board. These primitive skate boards were the beginning of the skate board revolution in our country. The boarders today are doing spectacular routines with their boards. They probably wouldn't believe how the people of the 50's could manipulate those early primitive boards.

There were three freeways in Los Angeles. The forth freeway, the Harbor freeway, was opened when I was in high school in Torrance. Hollywood was fairly close and very accessible to the public. Some students from our high school newspaper went to Hollywood to interview Lucile Ball. You could frequently see Danny Thomas in a restaurant in Santa Monica at the corner of Santa Monica Boulevard and Ocean Drive. Other movie stars could be seen around Hollywood and Malibu. We saw Byre Ives washing his car in Malibu. We frequently saw Jeff Chandler in Westwood.

One of our majorettes was elected Homecoming Queen. She was Japanese and had been interned with her family in a camp in Arizona during WWII. Today she is an artist and has a series of paintings which depict her experience in one of the internment camps. The paintings are truly wonderful. He name is Mary Yoshioka.

Interestingly, a medical school classmate of mine, Steve Kobiashi, was also interned with his family during WWII. At that time (1941) his father was a general surgeon in a city (Inglewood) not far from Torrance. Steve is a great guy and became a general surgeon. He practiced general surgery in northern California.

Modified cars were everywhere. These were the true "Happy Days" of the 50's. The music of the 50's would become timeless. We had a number of interesting extracurricular events while I was in school there. For instance, one night three of us were driving to Tijuana, Mexico to close a deal on the purchase of some cows that my friend was buying there. He was driving his pickup truck. Of course, we were stopped at the border. Two of us were 17 and were not allowed into Mexico without a parent. Unfortunately, the third guy did not qualify as a parent. They took us into a smoke-filled holding room which was full of rather suspicious looking people. Of course, our imaginations told us they all were smuggling drugs or running guns into Mexico. Our imaginations were probably right on a few of them.

We waited there for a couple of hours. Finally, they searched and interviewed us. Somehow, we convinced them we were buying cows south of the border (I don't necessarily recommend using that as a reason to be going to Mexico at 2 am in the morning). They eventually let us go north to San Diego.

I pretty much forgot about the whole incident until one day at home I heard my mother let out this loud scream. She called for my dad to look a letter she had just opened. It couldn't have anything to do with me could it? You guessed it, the letter was from the US Department of Immigration. The letter began, "Dear Mr. and Mrs. Emery: Your son was recently apprehended at the US Mexican border at 2 am on 4/11/56 attempting to enter Mexico. He was under aged. He and his friends told us he was going into the country to buy cows. Fortunately, he was unarmed. We did not find any drugs in their procession. We strongly suggest that you monitor your son's activities more closely, etc., etc. ". Well, that went over like a lead balloon. The most difficult part of the whole incident was when I was trying to explain to my parents what we planned to do with the cows. Since the plan was conceived by my friend, I actually had no idea what he planned to do with the cows.

I played football and baseball at Torrance High. There were college scholarship bound athletes in football, basketball, and baseball at Torrance.

I played running back at Torrance High School

The year before I got there a football halfback named Skip Smith had been named the national co-player of the year for football along with Billy Cannon (future star at LSU). He was a superb athlete and a good student. He was also the best street fighter in southwest Los Angeles County. He did not like to fight, but circumstances at times forced him into fighting. The fights usually involved him defending his friends against off campus bad boys trying to intimidate or hurt them. Torrance was close to some rough parts of L.A. County (Long Beach, Wilmington and San Pedro). Once his reputation had been established in that area, every tough guy around wanted to fight him. This was a real mistake on their part. Skip was never hurt and he was undefeated on the street. He actually seemed a little embarrassed that he had to go around doing these things. Those who tried to tackle him on the football field quickly understood how he got his reputation on the street.

He went to Nebraska on a football scholarship and later transferred to UCLA. At UCLA he was a powerful running back. I did not know him at Torrance, but we were to spend many hours together on the UCLA football practice field and in the Phi Delta Theta fraternity. We became lifelong friends and are still in contact today.

In 1956, my friend and I went to visit UCLA on a recruiting trip for football. We met the coaches in their office at Spalding field. There was a Who's Who list of coaches in the office. "Red" Sanders was the head coach. Several of the other coaches there would become well known college and professional coaches. I actually was going to do surgery on one of them later in my life (I operated on one of the coaches in the room years later when he was head coach of the San Diego Chargers). The coaches were reviewing films of Stanford. They noticed something in the footwork of Stanford's quarterback. When his feet were in a certain position they thought he would drop back to pass. One of the UCLA linebackers would yell "Omaha" when he saw this and he and an end would blitz the quarterback. UCLA won in a close game. This game would become known as the "Omaha" game in the annuls of UCLA football.

Stanford's best end was Gary Van Gaulder from Fresno, California. A huge coincidence was that Gary and I were to be in the same urology residency 12 years later at the University of Oregon Medical School. This was another one of the striking coincidences in my life.

That fall our Torrance High School team played football in the Bay League. We had good players, but ended up with a losing season. My friend, Tom, had a good season and would go on to play end at Utah University. I had a pretty good season and would go on to play at UCLA.

I was elected commissioner of athletics for the spring sports of 1957. I was looking through the sports history chronicles of Torrance high school for a guest speaker for our spring banquet when I came across the name of Louis Zamperini. I researched his career as a Torrance athlete. He had grown up in Torrance and was a track star there. I called him and he consented to give our after-dinner speech. We sat together at the banquet. I found him to be a wonderful person. He was in his early 40's at that time.

Louis Zamperini was a track star at Torrance High School

As he spoke to us after dinner, an unbelievable story began to unfold. He had grown up in Torrance. He had been a track star at Torrance high in the 30s. He was in the 1936 Olympics in Germany. He ran in the middle-distance races. He met Adolf Hitler during the games. He went on to USC and set records in the middle distance running events. His times in these races were the record at USC for many years.

He served with the Army Air Corps in the Pacific during WWII as a lieutenant in a bomber crew. A plane he was in crash landed in the Pacific and he and two other crew mates had to survive for 47 days in a lifeboat. They were captured by the Japanese and put into a POW camp. He was forced to run against the Japanese runners, despite the fact that he had been tortured and starved in the camps. He repeatedly challenged their runners. He returned to Torrance after the war and faced other challenges in his life. He was converted to Christianity during a Billy Graham revival meeting in a tent in Los Angeles. They remained friends throughout their lives. Louie became an inspirational speaker. We heard this remarkable story of his life that night of the sports award banquet in the spring of 1957.

The story of his life was eventually told in the bestselling book "Unbroken" and the movie of the same name. The movie was directed by Angelina Jolie. Angelina, of course, is the hugely talented and popular movie star of our era. Her humanitarian work throughout the world is well known.

Louie is known as the best USC athlete of all time. He was seen in a recent (August 28, 2012) Sports Illustrated article featuring the quarterback at USC and USC football program. There is a picture of Louie on the cover of this issue of Sports Illustrated. Louie was 93 years old at the time this picture was taken.

I worked at a Florist Shop (Windsor's Florist) in Redondo Beach during the summers and on weekends when I was in high school in Torrance. My high school friend, Bill Reynolds, worked there also. Now, I'll tell you, that job was the source of many funny stories for me. I'll tell you of one of these.

Bill and I worked in the back of the store for the most part. We were taught how to make corsages, flower arrangements, funeral wreaths and floral funeral blankets. All of these items, of course, were sold for a lot of money. Can you imagine two "goon" high school students selling our artistic creations for money? One day, the owner told a customer we were graduates of the USC school of horticulture. Come on man, give us a break. I also delivered flowers all over southwest Los Angeles County.

One time, we had a request to decorate the Glass Chapel in Palos Verdes for a wedding. This chapel is quite well known and is the site or many very nice weddings. Governor (of California) Earl Warren's daughter was married there during that period of time. Bill and I helped with the various flower arrangements necessary. Those arrangements included flowers for the front of the chapel, flowers for the end of the pews, a bouquet for the bride, corsages for the bridesmaids, and rose bud lapel pieces for the men in the wedding. We also had a white roller for the main isle.

The person who owned the shop wasn't known for his punctuality. You can can guess where I'm going and it isn't going to be pretty. As we were moving along with the wedding flowers, time was getting short. Finally, we had everything ready. The only problem was it was 30 minutes before the wedding and I had to drive from Redondo Beach out through Palos Verdes to the chapel. In addition to that they sent me alone to do the job. I have some advice for you----don't try to do that.

The only good thing about the whole deal was the fact that I didn't get arrested for speeding or wreck the truck. When I got to the chapel the parking lot was full, the people were sitting in the chapel and the minister was standing in front of the chapel. I was so focused on the job at hand that I wasn't sure what the minister said to me, but it wasn't very nice.

Have you ever tried to decorate a church for a wedding by yourself with the guests already sitting in the pews? It's not easy, especially for a completely untrained dork. I had to devise a plan of attack on the fly.

What do you think of this plan? I put the flowers on the end of the pews first, realizing that I better not have to walk on the white runner to get the flowers on the end of the pews. Then I put the flower baskets in the front of the chapel. Then I put the white roller down the center isle. Then I gave the men their rose bud lapel arrangements. I did that so one of them wouldn't deck me before I got to the women's stuff. I then gave the bridesmaids their corsages. I thought they wouldn't yell at me if I hadn't gotten the bride yet. I then gave the beautiful bride her beautiful bouquet as the last delivery. She smiled nervously. Remember, this is a very famous and distinctive place to be married and is still in use today.

Thank God I didn't have to pin a lapel rose bud on the minister. I simply gave the father of the bride the bill for the church decoration. He looked so nice with his rose bud in his lapel (surely, he was seething underneath that lapel rose bud).

Then I got the hell out of there after the minister had a few choice words for me. I have no idea if the father of the bride ever paid the flower decoration bill. I'm not sure I would have.

I played in a High School All Star football game that summer after we graduated from high school. Coach Cardura from Redondo Beach was our head coach. He was a wonderful coach. I met so many players I had played against during the previous year. Lynn Hoyem was our quarterback

I was designated to play halfback in the game. Shortly after the game started one of our linebackers was hurt. Coach Cardura asked if I would play linebacker also. I was happy to. I played halfback and linebacker for the rest of the game. I had a good game. The guy I replaced early in the first quarter received the defensive player of the game (his number was 31 and mine was 51). Coach Cardova was upset about the defensive player of the game thing. It didn't bother me. I enjoyed playing both ways.

One of the UCLA coaches came into the locker room after the game and said, "You're going to play at UCLA". Even though I wasn't going to eventually get much varsity game time at UCLA, it was nice to hear that from him at the time.

Chapter 4

UCLA

UCLA is in a beautiful part of Los Angeles. Hollywood is just to the northwest of UCLA. To the west is Brentwood, the Rivera Country Club, Will Rodgers State Park and the Pacific Ocean. A little further to the southwest is Santa Monica

UCLA is, as you know, one of the best academic centers in the country. I was very impressed when I first saw the school. It was founded in 1923. The original buildings reflect the architecture of that time. They are much more modern in appearance than Cal-Berkley or the University of Washington. There were no freeways around there then and I simply drove up Sepulveda Blvd to get to the school

The academic atmosphere at UCLA was excellent. Most of the departments there were well known throughout the country. The theater arts department there was especially good. For years the graduates of this program have made great contributions to the movie industry. On many occasions, the Hollywood producers would come to UCLA and USC to get seconds and stand-ins for their movies. Several players and a coach from UCLA were seen as soldiers on a train in the World War II movie "From Here to Eternity". One of our coaches was a stretcher bearer was a stretcher bearer in the movie "The Fly".

In 1958 I took a course in international politics. Our professor told us the United States would be extensively involved politically and militarily in Southeast Asia during the next 10 to 15 years. Once again, I had no idea I would be sitting in the middle of all that 10 years later in Vietnam. In fact, I would be sitting in the middle or the biggest battle of that war in 1968. I began UCLA as geology major. I became interested in anatomy and physiology and would change my major to pre-med about a year later.

I encountered some unusual events as I spent hours in the classrooms there. One of those unusual events I experienced was in a comparative anatomy class. We were supposed to bring in a sample of a bug, worm, lizard, or some type of small animal to class and compare their different anatomies. I had trouble finding such a creature. My mother finally caught a lizard in the driveway outside our house in Redondo Beach. The only problem was that the she poured bleach on the lizard and then cut it in half with a rake as she captured it. I wasn't about to hand in a half of a shrunk-up lizard for my project. I loved the fact that she had tried to help me. I finally found some bugs and pasted them on a board and turned it in.

I guess another guy also had trouble finding anything to turn in as a specimen. He brought in a mannose jar, filled it with milk and put some tadpoles in there. They were swimming around in the milk. He labeled his specimen "elephant sperm". The instructor was not overly impressed, but the rest of the students were in stiches. One guy said," I knew those things had eyes, but you could have fooled me with those mouths".

I hope I can relate this story clearly for you. I took an anthropology class during my first year. One day we were shown a film of an Aborigines' ritual initiation rite for males as they ascended into manhood. The film was astonishingly interesting and shocking. Before the film began the professor asked anyone who was squeamish at the site of blood to leave the room.

The film began by showing an aborigines village in the desert of Australia. All the people were nude except for small loin cloths. A male teenager was placed over the backs of two men, who were on all fours on the ground (sort of a make shift operating table). Two other men held the boy in place. A man then took a sharp rock and cut this boy's penis longitudinally on its underside from the urethral opening down to the base of the penis. The penis was now split into two sides with some tissue at the top side of the shaft holding the two halves together. The finished product looked sort of like an upside hot dog bun. This meant the boy would now urinate through a hole (urethral opening) at the base of the penis.

If you ladies out there want your men to do something major for you, threaten them with this initiation rite. They may not do what you want them to do, but you will get their attention for the rest of their lives.

At this point of the movie there was a loud thud heard in the back of the classroom. The professor turned on the lights to find that some guy had fainted and was lying on the floor at the rear of the room. The guy was dragged out of the room.

The professor turned the movie back on. The movie concluded by showing a few drops of blood coming from the cut in this boy's penis. I can't remember how the professor explained how these people could do this without the person bleeding significantly. If this were done to one us, there would be a significant blood loss and the person might go into shock.

I think I can tell you how they could get away with this primitive surgery. These people live in the desert of Australia and are exposed to extreme variations in temperature. In the winter months (our summer months in the northern hemisphere) the temperatures approach near freezing levels. These people have developed a specialized vascular "counter current" mechanism that allows them to survive at these low temperatures during the winter. This counter current mechanism is a vascular phenomenon where the vascular (blood vessel) system controls the flow of blood to the appendages of the body in a special way. This vascular system allows these people to shunt their arterial blood flow away from their appendages (arms, legs, ears, nose and penis) to their central core in order to preserve their internal body heat and, there by, keep their vital organs functioning.

In these Aborigines teenagers there was less blood flow to the penis during the cold weather. Their body was preserving heat to the core of the body where the vital organs are located. If you cut their penis then there would be minimal bleeding. They therefore can do this primitive surgery on the penis without significant bleeding. If you made this cut in the summer, when the temperature was much higher, the bleeding would be more severe because of the increased blood supply to these appendages.

I feel safe in saying that it is likely no urologist has seen anything to compare with this aborigines' initiation ritual. Yes, we urologists all have seen many self-inflicted or accidental penile injuries. None of these were done by the person cutting their penile urethra with a sharp rock as part of an initiation ritual, where the evolutionary development of a vascular countercurrent mechanism allowed this primitive surgery to be done without significant bleeding. If another urologist has seen anything this unusual I would like to hear from him.

As a side note on a related issue, is the fact that the soldiers of WW1 would periodically have to go through a "short arm" inspections. This referred to the fact they were having their shortest appendage (the penis) inspected. If there was a purulent substance (pus) dripping from their penis, they were assumed to have gonorrheal infection of the penile urethra. This was treated by soaking a metal rod in bismuth and pushing it up their penile urethra. The procedure, itself, could be fatal if the urethra was torn and the soldier developed sepsis. This proved to be somewhat a deterrent for some of these soldiers to seek the company of local ladies engaged in the prostitution industry. Many decided to take the risk.

These ex-WW1 soldiers, who were treated with that method showed up in our VA urology clinics years later with severe scarring of their penile urethra. These patients required imaginative surgery to correct this severe problem. Some of them actually were treated exactly in the same manner as seen in this in this imitation rite of these Aborigines men as a preliminary surgery for their eventual repair. When reconstructive surgery was not effective in correcting their penile urethral scar the result would be a totally incised penile urethra with an opening in their perineum to urinate through. This is exactly how these Aborigines men ended up.

When I use the word appendage I'm not implying that these men walked using their penis. I did meet one guy who insisted he used his for a cane.

That year (1957), the UCLA football was fulfilling a sanction the NCAA had placed on them for an infraction of the college rules from a year previously. This a sanction dictated that their senior players could only play half of the games. Despite this sanction coach Sanders led them to a winning season

Early in our freshman team practice we discovered we were short of guards. I volunteered to play guard, even though I had always been a running back up to that point in my football career. Bad idea! I stayed at that position for the next two years. As freshman, we played three games (Cal, USC, and Stanford). We won the Cal and Stanford games.

When we played USC, it was a different story. I had never seen so many High School All American football players in one place at one time in my life. They had five All Americans in the line and one or two in the backfield. Worse than that, I was playing guard (a position I had never played before) for the third time. You talk about on the job training, this was it. Even though I was knocked out of the game temporarily by one of their ends, I did semi-ok. They won the game by two or three touchdowns.

An interesting part of UCLA football at that time was the fact that the well-known Hollywood comedy star, Joe E. Brown, was a strong booster and supporter of the UCLA football program. He could be frequently be seen at football practices and hardly ever missed a game.

That fall my friends and I went through fraternity rush. My good friend, Bob (from San Diego and also on a football scholarship), and I pledged the Phi Delta Theta Fraternity. There were a lot of wonderful people in our fraternity. There was the usual harassment of pledges during the fall of that year. Our most challenging task occurred when we were left on Mulholland Drive, above Hollywood, one night dressed only in our underwear and shoes. We had to get back to our house at UCLA (crossing Sunset Blvd., etc.) without attracting too much attention or getting arrested. Try that one some time.

In the same fall of 1957 there was a national flu epidemic in the United States (one of the largest flu epidemics in U.S. history) and we all got it.

At the end of the semester we had the pleasure of going through "Hell week". I'll spare you all the gory details and hit only a few of the highlights of this memorable week. The week started with a party for the house members. The members had placed a tarp on the floor of the living room and covered it with chicken excrement that they had gotten from a local chicken farm.

Our first job for the week was to be to clean up the chicken shit in the living room. After that we began to paint the interior of the house. We were kept awake for seven days. As you know, this is a modern interrogation technique used by the U.S. military. All I can tell you is don't rely on the intelligence information you get from this torture method. As time goes on without sleep you become disoriented and "goofy". While we were painting the inside of the house I actually painted half way over a window. Another time I painted a little house on a window. This sleep deprivation was punctuated by numerous harassment issues, which included occasional paddling, general harassment and intolerable meals.

One night, after hell week we decided to go down to the Olympic auditorium in downtown Los Angeles for a night of professional wrestling. The wrestling arena ring was poorly lit and every time the wrestlers hit each other or fell in the ring a cloud of small insects would rise into the air. Mr. Moto, the reigning "bad guy" in professional wrestling, was on the schedule that night. When the card got to him he was doing his usual amount of eye gouging and pulling his opponent down by his trunks. All the wrestlers wore these colorful wool trunks. The crowd hated Mr. Moto. They were booing him loudly. We came up with a brilliant idea.

We decided to cheer for him. He picked this up immediately. Every time he did something illegal or just plain bad, we would cheer loudly. He began to bow to us as we were cheering him on.

Then the unbelievable happened! Some lady, sitting behind my friend, took a big round house swing with her fairly large purse and hit my friend on the top of his head. He slumped down in his chair. We thought he had a skull fracture. The crowd began to cheer loudly and continued to cheer even while we were checking to see if he was alive. He was severely stunned, but still alive and not bleeding. We made a fairly quick decision that this may not be the best place for us to spend our night out in Los Angeles. Mr. Moto expressed great disappointment as we were leaving (my friend staggering noticeably). We continued to cheer for Mr. Moto as we left the auditorium.

Another night in beautiful downtown L.A. We finally got home later that night. Our fraternity brother had almost completely recovered from the injury he had sustained because he rooted for Mr. Moto. Clearly, he had not done as well as Mr. Moto that night. I hope Mr. Moto appreciated our loyalty.

People hitchhiked commonly in those days. Skip Smith and I hitchhiked to Yosemite and back on one occasion. On another occasion we drove with our girlfriends to his father's trailer at Bullhead City, Arizona, on the Colorado River. At that time Bullhead City consisted of a few trailers on the river.

One evening his father and I were fishing out of a boat in the river (in a very wide part of the Colorado River with a very swift current) when it got dark. Every time we tried to get to shore we would hit a sand bar. When we hit the sand bar the boat would get stuck and would not move. When that happened I would ask, "What do we do now?" His answer was always the same, "Take that rope, get out of the boat and pull us off this sand bar". We're talking in December, in the middle of the dangerous Colorado River and he wants me to get out and pull the boat off the sand bar. What choice do I have (he is in his late 60's and has a bad heart)? So, I get out, take the rope, and start pulling. For a few steps the freezing water only comes to just above my boots. Then I step into a channel and the water is suddenly up to my waist or chest. Despite the fact that I'm waist deep in this fast moving, freezing cold river, Mr. Smith says, "Keep pulling". Finally, I pulled the boat off this sand bar.

Somehow, I get back into the boat and we start to drift down the river. He then starts the motor, and we take off for the shore. After moving a varying number of yards, the same thing happens again. There we are stuck on another sand bar. I say, "Ok, don't tell me, just hand me the rope". After several of these maneuvers we finally get to shore. All I can tell you is that if you are fishing out of a boat in the Colorado River at Bullhead City, try to get to shore while it's still light.

In the spring of 1958 at UCLA we had spring practice in football. I came down with mononucleosis (very common among college students and others who live in close contact with each other) and missed most of spring practice. I stayed at guard and was told I would be red-shirted the next year. That's not the best news I could get. I played freshman baseball that spring.

Sports medicine had not been developed at that time. Actually, sports medicine consisted of two players going on the field and dragging you back to the bench if you were a little dizzy after a hit on the field. Concussion screening consisted of someone asking you a series of questions. The questions were really not that hard (what day is it? etc.) If you answered some of the questions right you might be ready to go back into the game

We had an orthopedic surgeon as our football team physician. He was at all our games and many of our practices. Our head trainer was Ducky Drake. He was a nationally known head track coach at UCLA. The track stadium at UCLA is named after him. He was the best person you could imagine. He was a strong player's advocate. He was a role model for all of us. What he said was the last word. If he said you could not practice, you did not practice. If he said you did not play, you did not play. Most players were not anxious to hear they could not play.

On one occasion, I sustained a laceration at the outside corner of my right eye when I fell on a tackle's shoe cleat in practice. The doctor took me to the helmet storage shack on the field where he sewed up the laceration (a slightly different approach to the sports medicine procedures we see today). For you doctors out there, there were no disposable suture packs in those days. In fact, there were no disposable instruments, period. Instruments were stored in a covered pan full of a disinfectant (in the helmet shack). I'm not sure what type of suture he used, but I know he didn't use xylocaine for local anesthesia. I returned to practice when the doctor finished sewing me up.

This is a good one. One of our players was one of the best linemen in the United States. He was big for that day, fast and extremely strong. He was actually undefeated at guard during his years at UCLA. Call him Jack. One day near the end of practice I was playing against Jack. We were sort of coasting into the final minutes of practice. My fraternity brother, Lee, was playing behind me at linebacker (he was known as a con man in our frat house). He says "Let's get Jack". I did not know that "let's" really meant "me". Stupid me, I say, "Ok". He says, "I'll push you from the back and you hit him and we'll kick his ass". Notice the "we'll". He pushed me and I hit Jack. Unfortunately, when he pushed me my forearm went higher and I hit Jack right in the face. He went back to the huddle saying he was going to kill me. One of the players in the huddle said not to kill me because I was a good guy. I'm not sure Jack heard him. He came back up to the line of scrimmage. I knew what was coming. Fortunately, I blocked his forearm with my forearm (as I muttered "thank God"). I managed to finish the practice alive.

In the locker room Jack comes right up to me and gets in my face. Of course, I thought I would soon be on my way to the emergency room. Instead he said, "you see this cut on my face". I mean the cut was, at the most, microscopic in size. I said, "Yea, I see it". He says; "No one has ever cut me". I'm beginning to feel a little better. At least he probably isn't going to punch me.

Then says, "How did you do that". Man, what a relief. I'm having a problem coming up with an answer. I'm clearly not going to tell him that my fraternity brother pushed me from behind. Finally I say, "I must be faster than you, Jack". He looks at me with this funny look and walks off. Of course, we became good friends over the years as we both ended up in San Diego some years later.

My fraternity brother con-man, who talked me into that, ended up a multi-millionaire from oil and some sort of loan company. The last time I saw him was when Jack and I flew up to UCLA for a football reunion in my con man fraternity brother's airplane flown by his personal pilot!

On that flight I met a former tackle at UCLA who went on to the NFL and played center for the NY Giants. On the flight home from a professional game, when he was with the Giants, he had a stroke. What likely happened was that he was struck in the chest and may have developed a temporary cardiac arrhythmia and developed a clot in his left atrium. The clot then passed out of his heart to his cerebral circulation, giving him a stroke. The other possibility was that he may have developed a clot in his left atrium or ventricle from the contusion. Such an injury was more likely to happen in another activity (car accident) other than football. Again, I wonder if another doctor has seen this type of injury in football game. Fortunately, this player recovered completely from the stroke.

One day, the back of my head on the right side turned numb and stayed that way for a few months. It was not until I reached medical school a few years later did I figure out what had happened. The right greater occipital nerve, which exits the skull in the back on the right side, had been stretched severely and lost its sensory function. That is very close to a serious injury. After a few months the feeling returned to the back of my head indicating that the nerve hadn't been interrupted completely.

A very tragic event happened to me when my friend, a tackle, sat on my pants in the locker room. My plastic bridge with a single front tooth on it was in my pants pocket. I pulled the bridge out of my pocket and discovered that the tooth had broken off the bridge. Here I was with the plastic bridge in one hand and the plastic tooth in the other hand.

I walked around the campus for a few weeks holding my front tooth in my mouth with my tongue. Despite this obvious disability, I tried to act semi-intelligent as I went through my classes. After a while a local dentist put the tooth on a metal bridge and I was soon back in business. That metal bridge was horrible to wear.

During the year, the scholarship athletes were given various jobs around the campus. During the summer we were given jobs in various industries around Los Angeles County. That summer I was assigned to work for the Union Oil Company oil field in Wilmington, California. The Willington field is located on an island (Terminal Island) north of Long Beach. I ended up working on a "bullshit" crew. That's a crew that works on existing wells as opposed to a drilling crew, which is involved in the drilling of new wells. The bullshit crew is involved in the repair of problems that occur in existing wells. The crew exists of three or four men and "pusher". The pusher is the boss of the crew.

The crew works on a portable oil rig which has been set up over a well. The rig has a floor and a tower. Two men work on the floor and one in the tower (on a platform at the top of the rig known as the derrick). The pusher usually runs the motor that controls a small elevator that goes up and down the tower. Under ground the oil is pumped up a length of pipes that run from the bottom of the well to the surface. Inside the pipes are metal rods that run up and down inside the pipes and are connected to the pump apparatus at the bottom of the well. You can see the top end of these rods connected to the horse-like machine at ground level that moves up and down and has a large counter balance on it. All over the field you can see these horse-like machines going up and down as they are pumping oil to the surface.

So here comes the new college kid to work on the bullshit crew. Many of the men on these crews are from Texas and Oklahoma and came west during the blue-collar migration to California that occurred in the late 40's and the 50's.

These guys had some unusual forms of entertainment. One of these was a "coon bagging contest". At a group picnic they would put a raccoon in a tree, and then divide into two man teams. One guy would shake the tree and the other guy would try to catch the falling raccoon in a gunny sack. The raccoon would frequently bite the second guy on his arm or leg or worse. It helped that they pretty well anesthetized with alcohol.

The first thing you notice in the men in this oil field is that a few of them have various parts of their fingers missing. It doesn't take long to figure out how they lost them. If someone accidently drops one of those pipes there goes one, or part of one, of your fingers. I eventually ended up working in the derrick of the rig. They really enjoyed running that elevator fast toward me. Despite a few of these obvious disadvantages, I really enjoyed working there with these guys.

There was a guy named "Frenchie" who worked there. One of UCLA's great linebackers had worked there earlier. He later played for years for the Baltimore Colts. Apparently one day he threw Frenchie from a dike on Terminal Island into the ocean after Frenchie had played a practical joke on him.

One day, Frenchie came up to me and said he had he had an idea. He would tell everyone that I had been made a "pusher" because I was so well educated. The pushers of these crews had spent years in the field to reach the position of pusher. Stupid me, I agreed to do it (not a good move). As the day went on, I kept getting more and more evil looks from the workers. At the end of the day we all cleaned up in a company locker room. There was dead silence when I came in. Pretty soon a worker came up to me and said "I am the representative of the local Union 7642 and I need to talk to you". Thank God, Frenchie came up and told the other worker what we had done. Frenchie was the only one in the room laughing at his big joke. Fortunately, I had enough sense not to laugh!

Back to UCLA football. In the summer of 1958 coach Sanders died suddenly. Everybody was saddened. Coach George Dickerson was named head coach. He became ill after three games into the 1958 season and Coach Bill Barnes was named head coach. He was an assistant coach under coach Sanders. He literally had days to prepare for our next game. He did a great job.

UCLA 1959

That year I was informed that I would be "red shirting" for the year. "Red shirting" is an experience that many players in many sports have done in our country through the years. Basically, you are not eligible to play for a year and you play on a redshirt team, which is like a practice squad. In the daily practices, you play against one to three varsity teams. During the week, you play much more football than the varsity players play. On game day, you usually are in the stands watching the game. You do not travel with the team for away games.

During that year you were encouraged to lift weights and get heavier, hopefully from added muscle and not fat. There were no steroids in those days. If you took in a lot of calories you would add body fat, perhaps not a bad thing if you were a lineman. The UCLA teams were characterized by speed and quickness. There weren't any fat guys around. I maintained the orangutan theory and stayed lean and quick. I was much lighter than our line coach would have liked. When he asked me how much I weighed I would add 20 lbs. to my actual weight and tell him I had heavy bones. He seemed ok with that explanation.

We had two a day practices in August. It was over 90 degrees and there was significant smog in the air around the Los Angeles area. The smog made breathing labored. We literally lost pounds of fluid during the day. We replaced water, but it was usually after practice. At that time, there was no real understanding of fluid and electrolyte physiology of the human.

Fortunately, we did not take salt tablets. Salt ingestion would only worsen our electrolyte problem, as we will soon see. The conditions were even worse in the central parts of our country where the heat and humidity were higher.

I will use these conditions to discuss some of the problems we can develop from vigorous activity in hot weather. Clearly, these problems can develop in any of the vigorous activities we do in hot weather. This is not a condemnation of playing football in hot weather, it's simply that I am using this sport to discuss the problems we face in exerting ourselves in hot weather. That allows me to bring up some issues you may not be familiar with.

Three problems can develop under the circumstances of vigorously exerting ourselves in hot weather. The first problem is overheating of the body. As your internal temperature rises with exertion the overheated blood is brought to the surface of your body and the body heat radiates into the air helping to cool your body and the fluid (sweat) on the surface of your skin evaporates into the air helping to cool your body.

The ability of your body to cool itself is greatly governed by your body mass to surface area ratio. In large animals, there is a relatively smaller surface area to weight ratio. An elephant has a large body mass, but in comparison has a relatively small surface area when compared to it's huge weight. It is hard for the elephant to lose body heat from the limited surface area of their body compared to their large body mass, which can produce a lot of heat in their internal body. A hummingbird, on the other hand, has a very large surface area when compared to their body weight. It is much easier for them to lose heat from the surface of their body.

So here we are exerting ourselves playing football in hot humid weather. You have greatly reduced your surface area to body mass ratio by wearing a helmet and uniform. This reduces your effective surface area to lose heat from. Physiologically you are converting yourself toward a dog, who has only a small area to lose heat from. Not only that, you are wearing a material (cotton) that becomes saturated with a fluid. With these wet clothes on you further reduce your body's ability to lose heat by radiation and evaporation. Your internal body temperature can elevate to critical levels. You are setting yourself for a heat stroke.

So who are the players most likely to suffer a heat stroke on the football field. You guessed it, it's the big heavy lineman. If they have gained weight to enhance their abilities, they are in even worse shape with regard to heat loss by voluntarily reducing their surface area to body mass ratio. While wearing football uniforms, they have further reduced their surface area from which they can lose heat. These are the players more likely to develop heat stroke. They get yelled at because they run slow. The skinny defensive backs are much better off in terms of their surface area to body weight ratio and they are not in as much risk to develop heat stroke.

Today, many improvements have been made to try to correct this problem. Uniform materials have improved by allowing body to lose heat from radiation. Fans are being used on the sidelines to enhance evaporative heat loss. Playing time has been reduced form the whole sixty minutes to much less time of playing. Fluids are given generously.

As recently as the late 50's these improvements had not been made. In addition to that, you were not allowed to drink water while playing or practicing. At times, you were considered "weak" if you had to drink water. The only thing "weak" about this idea was the brain of the guy who came up with the idea in the first place. In addition to that you might be given salt tablets, which is almost as bad as not drinking water! Somebody suggested that we suck on rocks to help us hydrate with our own saliva, if, by chance, we had any saliva left at the time. That guy who came up with this idea was dumber than the guy who thought you were weak if you needed water

This brings us to the second problem you can developed under the conditions we have been considering, and that is the fact that you can develop severe fluid losses from the sweating of your body during exercise in hot weather. This fluid loss is greatly increased with vigorous exercise. This loss is even greater at higher temperatures. This problem carries the same degree of risk of illness and even death as the problem of uncontrolled overheating does. Your total body water decreases from water losses you develop during vigorous activity, especially in hot weather. This results in dehydration. As this dehydration continues, eventually your blood volume decreases. As your blood volume decreases, your blood pressure drops and the perfusion of blood to your vital organs is decreased. You will die in hypovolemic shock and progressive organ shutdown.

Today this fluid loss condition is treated well in professional and college sports, where there is a sports medicine doctor and their staff present. You are kept hydrated with water or sport drinks during the game. If your fluid losses exceed your ability to keep yourself hydrated orally, you are given the appropriate intravenous solutions in the locker room.

For the rest of us out there exercising without the presence of a sports medicine doctor, we must keep ourselves hydrated. Stop, rest and hydrate. As you expend energy you also will need to take an energy source such as carbohydrates and fats or, less desirably, proteins (it takes longer to convert them into an energy source).

The third problem you can develop while exercising is an electrolyte abnormality. As you exercise you lose a lot of fluids through sweating. The concentration of sodium chloride (NaCl) or salt in your sweat is initially low. You are losing a lot more water through sweating than salt. The result of this is the fact you will develop a higher concentration of sodium chloride (NaCl) or salt in your body and blood stream. This electrolyte abnormality is called <u>hypernatremia</u>. As this condition worsens with continuing water losses you can become lethargic, confused, could potentially develop seizures and eventually die.

During this process, you can manifest some salt crystallization on your skin. This does not mean you are losing significant amounts of salt. This only means that the concentration of salt in your sweat is increasing as your body is trying to conserve water. Do not take salt tablets. You simply will make your condition worse. The single most important principal is to keep yourself hydrated with water or some water containing drink.

During a recent Olympics, a female marathon runner collapsed near the finish line and tried to crawl to the finish line in a stroke-like position. She surely was suffering from severe dehydration and electrolyte imbalance (hypernatremia). She probably had poured the water on her head to cool herself rather than drinking it!!! She was fine after she drank water, which corrected her dehydration and electrolyte imbalance.

If you are exercising and losing water, you need to hydrate with water and take in some small amount of salt. The water should have natural sugar in it to provide you with caloric needs. You could drink a natural sugar sports drink. You also simply drink a natural sugar Kool-Aid and eat a few potato chips.

In 50's and prior to that, people simply did not understand the basics of fluid and electrolyte physiology. This understanding would not come until the early 60's when the basics of fluid and electrolyte physiology were first described by Dr. Isadore Edelman at UCSF Medical School.

Can you ever over hydrate yourself? Yes, you can and that problem can be quite dangerous and even fatal. When you drink too much water beyond your natural body needs your serum sodium concentration will begin to drop. If this process continues you will begin to feel strange and disoriented. Beyond that you can begin to have seizures and can eventually expire from a severe electrolyte imbalance. This condition is called "water intoxication". The condition was seen most commonly in medicine as a complication of a transurethral resection of the prostate when water was used as an irrigating solution.

Under ordinary circumstances the body will not reach this point naturally. You have to force this amount of overhydration by impulsive drinking of water or by administering inappropriate intravenous solutions. We have developed such a focus on the importance of hydration that some well-meaning patients can overdo it. If they drink more water than their body can balance appropriately they can develop this problem. You should be aware of this.

Football has received a lot of attention recently because of the possibility of sustaining a head injury. Football is a rough contact sport and there is the potential to sustain blunt trauma to the head. When you get a blow to the head your brain is moved quickly within its fluid suspension of cerebral spinal fluid within a delicate sack around your brain. This blow and sudden movement of the brain causes the brain to slam against the skull. This slamming of the brain against the bony skull is what produces the brain injury. Within the skull this type of injury can result in a contusion (deep bruise) of the brain tissue or a tearing of blood vessels in the brain or on its surface, resulting in bleeding in the brain or on its surface. Either of these events can produce a concussion or worse at the time of the injury.

As a group, these injuries are referred to as <u>closed head injuries</u> (injuries that occur without a skull fracture). This type of injury is not exclusive to the sport of football. The same injury can occur in any sport or activity where there is the potential to sustain a blow to the head. The sports include soccer, basketball, baseball, gymnastics, skiing, polo and a long list of other sports. The activities include almost anything you are doing that could result in your head hitting a hard surface. That means all of us who are just walking around.

Great improvements have been made in the design of football helmets. Changes in the rules have tried to make conditions safer for the players. At this point in time, football players have better head injury protection than in most other sports, with the exception of race car drivers.

Some of the most forceful blunt traumas to the brain occurs when you fall backwards and you whip lash your head onto a hard surface. Your head is traveling at a high level of speed when it hits this immovable object (the ground). This occurs not infrequently in football, basketball, baseball, soccer, skate boarding, boxing and other sports or any activity where you can fall over backwards. Again, that would be any of us simply walking around. The back of your skull is thinner than the front of your skull and therefore, more susceptible to fracture. The back of the brain is where the visual and balance centers are located.

In the modern game of football the helmets are more protective, necks are stronger, and the face masks are more protective. These facts encourage the player to use his head as a battering ram. This idea developed in the mid-sixties and beyond. Spearing a player with your head is a bad idea on the football field. If someone spears another player he should leave the game and/or be suspended if he continues to engage in this dangerous maneuver. We are slowly addressing this problem. The most important change would be the instruction of a low head injury way of playing the game. More changes in the rules will happen in the future.

The next most vulnerable part of the body in a football player, or for anyone for that matter, is his neck. Our upright posture predisposes us to neck trauma. Most neck fractures in this country occur with non-sports related activities. Most football players try to protect their necks by developing the strength of the muscles of their neck. Once again, if you want to break your neck go spear someone on a football field.

If steroids are used, the potential for injury is magnified. The player taking them experiences a greater than normal weight gain from muscle tissue and fluid retention. This disrupts the body weight to bone mass ratio of their body out of balance. Their weight is far greater than the bones were designed to support. This means the bones are at greater risk for fracture. If the person taking the steroids experiences thinning of the bones (another potential side effect of taking steroids), this also increases the risk of bone fractures.

Steroids also have the side effects of changing your personality to one who has a higher level of aggressiveness, hypersexuality and viciousness. These side effects will result in abnormal behavior that can result in the user getting into more trouble with personal relationships and the law. We have seen repeated examples of this among those individuals who have used steroids in the sporting world.

With all this talk about the risks of playing football, is there anything good about playing this sport? I suppose it depends on your outlook on the sport. In my opinion, football is a great game to play if you if you are inclined to do so. Stop anytime you're not enjoying it.

The game teaches you that hard work and discipline can produce positive results. It is a game in which all the players are involved in each play. This teaches you the importance of teamwork. You are taught to work hard for the success of someone else. You are taught to protect your teammates from the aggression of the players on the opposing team.

Most importantly, it teaches you a systematic approach to problem solving and performance. In the game of football there are a great number of coordinated offensive and defensive maneuvers that one team can make against the other team. After every play, you meet and decide what maneuver you can do to be successful on the next play. The other team is doing the same thing. The plans for intricate play making are more complex than in other sports. These plans have to be executed well to achieve success.

Football is definitely a game that depends extensively on careful preparation and then good execution based on that preparation. Most businesses and professions depend on these same policies to be successful. If you have played this game these habits can be second nature to you.

Let's apply this to my profession. Was I a better surgeon because I played football? Yes, I was, because these principles of playing the game were ingrained in me since I was a young person. Careful preparation and good execution are the hallmarks of good outcomes from surgeries. An anesthesiologist once told me that he never saw me doing a surgery where I had not made it clear to him what the problems and objectives of the surgery were in the preoperative assessment I had given to him prior to the surgery. He said that was not always the case with other surgeons.

Obviously, the game of football has changed since I played it. I can only say that it was an important contributor to my abilities as a doctor and surgeon.

Playing baseball also had a positive effect on my ability as a surgeon. I played in the infield at third base. Infielders are said to have "soft hands". They work with the ball not against it.

Having soft hands is a definite asset in surgery when it comes to handling organs and tissues inside the body. Infielders are used to getting things done quickly and accurately. This quality I'm sure carried over into my practice in surgery. I was always looking for ways to get things done quickly and accurately when evaluating and treating my patients.

The early part of the 20th century you could not make the rank of general in the Army if you had not played football at West Point. The maneuvers in football can closely resemble military maneuvers. Generals Eisenhower, MacArthur, Patton and others had all played football at West Point. President Eisenhower was once asked what he did at West Point to which he responded "I played football and got demerits".

Young players today start the game in a very organized manner under the guidance of, for the most part, untrained adults. Unfortunately, these adults are usually not familiar with the instruction of "injury reduction football". This is the biggest danger in youth football today. These youth football coaches should have to attend a course on injury reduction before they are allowed to coach.

As I mentioned the game has changed since we played in the 50's and 60's. In the early 50's my friends and I watched two professional teams play an exhibition game at Laidely field in Charleston, West Virginia. The players were carrying their own bags with all their equipment in them. The equipment appeared to be older than the equipment we were using in high school. This was a far cry from what professional football is today.

The saddest change in professional football is that it has become a game of "me". It is no longer a game of "us". Entertaining antics have replaced the team concept of the game. This may be the beginning of the end of this American team sport.

Back to UCLA football. In 1959 we played against Syracuse the year they became National Champions. As red-shirt players, we read their scouting report and were preparing to run their offense and defense against the varsity teams. The varsity wore white cotton jerseys and the red shirt team wore red vests on the UCLA practice field. Nobody had a number on their jerseys. Pretty soon one of the coaches came up to me and gave me a red vest with the number 44 on it. He said," John, this week you are Ernie Davis". Ernie Davis was a great, soon to be All American, sophomore running back at Syracuse. In no way was my running style similar to his, although I had a sprained ankle which made me have a loping running style. Despite the fact that the whole varsity team was trying to tackle me all week, it was kind of fun to be Ernie for a week.

Those of us who follow football know the story of Ernie Davis. His life story has become legendary in the annuals of American football. He was a great All-American halfback at Syracuse. Near the end of his college career he was diagnosed as having a fatal blood disease. This wonderful young man fought this fatal illness with great courage and dignity. He was drafted by the Cleveland Browns. The Browns knew he would not be able to play for them when they drafted him. He was able to take the field as a Cleveland Brown before he passed away.

One day in the UCLA locker room our head trainer, Ducky Drake, was taping my ankle when he said to me, "John, did you ever think of getting into some other line of work"? I, of course, was shocked to hear that (not really!!). What he said helped me make my decision to not play football for my academic senior year and concentrate on getting into medical school.

Years later, when Ducky passed away the track stadium at UCLA was named Ducky Drake Stadium in honor of his life at this institution. The former mayor of Los Angeles, Tom Bradley, gave a eulogy for him at his funeral. Mayor Bradley had run track at UCLA for Ducky. This was one of the most memorable eulogies I have ever heard. At one point during his eulogy he asked anyone who had ever been taped up by Ducky to stand up. Nearly everyone in the church stood up. There were many tears in the eyes of those standing.

Coach Ducky Drake

Chapter 5

UCSF Medical School

One of the greatest things that ever happened to me was when I was accepted to the University of California at San Francisco Medical School in 1961. Nowhere in the world could one get a better medical education than in this medical school. The teaching of the fundamentals of medical care of patients was truly exceptional.

Our professors were excellent. Dr. Julius Comroe was a world's authority on the physiology of the lung. He wrote "The Lung", which was the first book to clearly describe the physiology of the lung. This was essential information for all doctors. Lung physiology comes into play in every illness.

Dr. Isledore Edelman was the first doctor to describe the fluid and electrolyte physiology of the human. His work was critical in the treatment of all illnesses. His assistant, Dr. Frank Gotch, put the details of this complicated subject into plane English. Dr. Edelman's publications on fluid and electrolyte physiology resulted in a drastic change in our attitude toward these problems and how to treat them. I have explained how it changed our treatment of abnormalities in fluid and electrolytes that occur in athletics.

Dr. J. Englebert Dunphy was a very well-known surgeon and an expert in wound healing. He was our Chief of Surgery. J. Hollingsworth Smith was a learned and sophisticated Chief of Medicine. His ability to teach this expansive subject was legendary. Dr. Charles Carmen was a great teacher in Internal Medicine. With these doctor teaching us, we were exposed to the latest advancements in medicine in the entire world. Many of them were the doctors who had described or developed these advancements.

My exposure to these men would be hugely influential in my performance as a doctor throughout my career in medicine. Our class was full of the most interesting, diversified, intelligent and humorous people one could imagine. We were very competitive toward each other until we had our first anatomy exam. Outside the door of the anatomy lab was a skeleton dressed up to look exactly like one of our anatomy professors. That opened the door for some of our more eccentric students to express themselves for four years.

Medical school wasn't supposed to be like this. It was supposed to be very competitive and full of tension. Forget that, this was going to be fun. And besides that, we were going learn an immense amount of information from excellent instructors. And besides that, we would help each other learn.

Our classmate, Earl Shultz, was an All-American basketball player from Cal. He was a good student and a very, very funny man. He became a successful radiologist in Escondido, California. He practiced there with another of our classmates, Don Alexander. Every time I think of Earl I just feel like laughing. What a pleasure to be around a person like him. Like I said we had a fun class! My classmates and I got to be around him for four years. As I mentioned earlier, he was a good friend of Jerry West's, who had grown up a few miles from us in West Virginia.

Others in our class included a naval officer, a naval pilot, a pool shark, a near professional comic and various other assorted unique and interesting people. Yes, we had many more traditional students. They basically had to sit back and observe the antics of the, shall we say, our more eccentric students.

My Friend, Steve Kobiashia, was in our class. Remember he had been interned with his family during WWII. Very funny man. He also was an excellent athlete. We spent many happy hours together. He became a general surgeon. He is the doctor I mentioned earlier, who was in an internment camp in WW II. His father was a doctor not far from where I went to high school.

We were divided into groups of 4-6 and took our lab classes and other subjects with this group of people. We had a physical exam course given at a local nursing home. Before we were turned loose on patients, we had to examine each other. When we got to the rectal exam part of the class, one of our very good looking and more expressive female students in the class said emphatically, "You perverts aren't touching me". Despite the fact that her group partners tried to explain to her that it was simply a scientific learning experience and professional maneuver, she did not budge from her stated position. She, on the other hand, was very happy to check their prostates!

I didn't have a whole lot of better luck when I went on to the ward for my first complete physical exam on a female patient. When I got to the rectal exam part I placed her on her side and began to do the rectal exam. As I was examining what I thought was in the rectal area when she said to me," Doctor, I know you are a doctor and all that, but I think you are in the wrong spot there". I had enough sense not to argue with her. After that, I made sure that I had a clear view of my destination. I did not want to make a wrong turn ever again.

We had an exchange with the U.C. Davis Veterinary School. We had them over to our school and they were shown some procedures the surgeons were doing, some of the early respirators we were using, some of the drugs we were using, etc. Overall interesting, but semi-boring.

Their show when they had us over was nothing short of spectacular. They showed us how they give a horse general anesthesia. They showed us how they manipulate the genes of plants to produce better crops. The highlight of the day was when they showed us how to collect a sperm specimen from a bull.

They brought this big bull into the room and proceeded to lock its feet to the floor. Some of us were getting the idea, but did not want to say anything. Then they got this large electrode and placed it into the bull's rectum. You got to be kidding me, they're actually going to do this. They turned on the juice and secretions and excretions came shooting out of every orifice of the bull. It was like the fourth of July, there were specimens everywhere. You simply had to put your specimen container under the appropriate orifice and you got the specimen you wanted. The bull was fine. Most of us felt sorry for the bull. I think there may have been a few of us who envied the bull.

Later in my career I saw a case of a couple who had connected themselves to wall sockets by way of electrodes in their rectums. This maneuver was done to enhance the feelings of their sexual experience. Apparently, their quality control was not as good as it was with the bull at UC Davis. In any event they did not fare nearly as well as the bull. The survival rate of this sexual enhancement hook-up was zero.

Remember I told you about my front tooth problem when I was playing football at UCLA. I went to see a dental student at the UCSF Dental School. He said he could make me a bridge for free. He didn't' tell me it was his first bridge. I mean it took this guy 6 months to make that damn bridge under the supervision of his instructor. The tooth kind of pointed out to the side a little, but it was good enough for government work. After all, it was free.

We spent a lot of our off-time on the weekends at a local bar near the school. If we had 50 cents for every hour we spent in that bar we could have paid our tuition easily ($125.00 a semester for an education at the best medical school in the world.)

A former Oakland Raider tackle was the bouncer at the bar. Fortunately, we only had one run-in with him. It occurred when a local neighborhood lady accused one us of stealing money from her purse, which was sitting on the bar. I mean we may have been poor, but one of us was certainly not going to steel some nice lady's money out of her purse when she went to the ladies' room. Especially when she asked us to watch her purse for her while she was gone. We had a little trouble convincing that ex-Oakland Raider tackle bouncer that we were honest guys, but, in the end, I think he believed us. He either believed us or just got tired of listening to us talk. Nobody got hurt and our friend went back to talking to that nice lady at the bar

We spent hours in that local bar trying to name the all-time baseball All-Star team. We had DiMaggio (he was from San Francisco and played for the Yankees for many years), Mantle, and Mays (playing for the San Francisco Giants at that time) were all vying for center field. We tried to put one of them at third, but that would have eliminated George Kell. First base (where they always put burned out outfielders) was already taken by Gehrig. I mean are you really going to put Joe Morgan at second base ahead of the Georgia peach, Ty Cobb? Come on!! Bill Dickey ahead of Yogi Berea at catcher.

Really??? There was no designated hitter at that time. You try this for yourself sometime. It's not as easy as you might think. It was clearly harder than any physiology class we had.

I'm getting to some more classroom stuff, but first I better tell you about this one incident that occurred in one of those downtown bars on a Friday night. Ok, my friend and I go down to one of those downtown San Francisco bars on a Friday night. We were planning to eat the horderves on the bar for dinner. Ok, he gets into a serious verbal altercation with a couple of guys in the bar. I have no idea what the issue was. I'm standing not far away exchanging pleasantries with some of the patrons, when he comes up and asks me to come with him. Apparently, these guys have invited him out into the alley behind the bar in order to settle this altercation man to man. I'd like at least to know what the altercation was about before I go with him. To this day I do not know what the problem was.

Ok, I follow him out into the alley. There stand these two guys in their designer sports coats in this dark alley behind this bar. To me they look like law students or young businessmen or something. The only problem is they each have a broken beer bottle in one of their hands. Ok, at UCLA I played with some very tough people, but I'm not crazy (at least, I thought I wasn't). Ok, he's going into psychiatry and I'm heading for urology, right. Ok, so I tell him, in a very convincing manner, to shut up and let me do the taking. Somehow, I convinced these guys that we are bigger chickenshits than they said we were. They finally agreed with me and we go back into the bar with our two new found friends.

Around this time the Haight Asbury district was about to heat up as hot spot in the social revolution of the 60's. This neighborhood was located just below the medical school. When we got there, it was a quaint low rent housing community. Some of our students lived there.

1967 was to be the summer of the "Flower Children" in the Haight Asbury district. This historically significant social event in U. S. history occurred in the summer of 1967. Unfortunately, I missed this colorful event. I was on a government sponsored trip to Chu Lai, South Vietnam.

Kezar Stadium was nearby and we could see part of the stadium from our anatomy lab. I could watch three of my ex-UCLA teammates play for the San Francisco 49ers in the stadium on Sundays. Golden Gate Park was not far away.

Yes, we did find time to go to some classes in medical school. I have already explained what our physical exam class was like. In one physiology class, we were studying the effects of various drugs on the physiology of the body. I volunteered to be studied after consuming a measured amount of Kentucky's finest Bourbon (a lot smoother than West Virginia "moonshine"). I can't remember what my physiologic measurements were, but I do remember it was an enjoyable class. One guy volunteered to take LSD. At the time LSD was a very popular drug to take for recreational use. It was sort of a time where everyone was trying to "expand their minds". Unfortunately, a lot of people had "bad trips", some of which ended in suicides

In November of 1963 our country experienced the tragic loss of President Kennedy. Our country was in shock. Everyone seemed to remember where they were when they got the news of President Kennedy's death. I was walking down a hall in San Francisco County Hospital.

When I was on the emergency room service as a junior student at San Francisco County Hospital we had a mass casualty situation occur. It happened one night when a group of Samoans were demonstrating fire dancing in a local church. It was in the winter and the church was poorly ventilated. Suddenly there was a flash explosion in the church. The injured patients were brought to our Emergency Room.

The patients from this church had first, second or third degree burns of the exposed parts of their bodies. Soldiers with heavy wool uniforms on experienced much less extensive burns than those people wearing lighter clothing.

There was another problem that developed among some of the patients who had burns of the upper respiratory tract. These upper respiratory tissues could swell up and create an obstruction to their airway resulting in possible suffocation. Those with severe upper respiratory tract burns were treated with plans to do a tracheostomy if necessary.

The patients with burns to their skin were placed on a burn treatment program. These programs had been greatly improved because of the understanding of fluid and electrolyte physiology provided by Dr. Edleman and others. Appropriate fluid replacement and antibiotics were essential parts of the early treatment of these burns. These treatments contributed greatly to the improvement in survival from burns to the body.

For us, as medical students, it was a chance to observe the management of a mass causality situation and the appropriate treatment of burn injuries. This observation of the management of a mass causality situation would be useful to those of us who would be going to the war in Vietnam a few years later.

I saw another event of what might be called "baptism by urinal". There was a hypertension medication which had the potential side effect of causing a psychotic reaction if you ate cheese while taking this medication. Sure enough, a large male patient on the medical ward ate a cheese sandwich while on this medication. He had a bad reaction and was going around the ward bopping the other patients on the head with his metal urinal (hence the name "baptism by urinal"). An emergency "patient out of control" code came over the loud speaker. We all ran up to the ward where these "baptisms" were taking place. It took four of us to get him down and give him a shot of Thorazine.

We saw our first case of the "Pickwickian Syndrome". This syndrome occurs in very heavy people when their body weight can affect their breathing so adversely that it causes respiratory failure. They can be fine at rest even though their respiratory muscles are working harder than normal to keep them breathing. When they are stressed, their need to breath increases and their respiratory muscles, because of the added work they need to do, cannot keep up with the increased demand. They then develop respiratory failure. They require respiratory support and are frequently in need of an endotracheal tube or tracheostomy and positive pressure ventilation until they get back to their resting level of energy requirements to breath. Without this support, they would go into a coma and eventually expire. This is true morbid obesity. Losing weight for them was truly lifesaving. Today they would be treated with bariatric surgery.

While I was on that service at the county hospital a young lady came in with "Guillian Barre's Syndrone". This condition is also known as a post infectious, ascending peripheral neuropathy. Basically, it occurs usually after minor viral illness or even vaccinations. A neuropathy begins in the lower body and ascends symmetrically upward in the body. You develop a weakness and eventual paralysis of the involved areas and it can then ascend to involve the arms, etc. If it reaches the nerves that control breathing, the respiratory muscles become paralyzed and you cannot breathe. At this point you need total respiratory support with an endotracheal tube (you may eventually require a tracheostomy) and positive pressure ventilation. At this stage, the condition can have a fatal outcome if the person does not have access to a respirator. This can happen, even today, if the diagnosis is delayed or the patient cannot get to a respirator in time. Usually the condition resolves completely and the person is left with little, if any, residual neurologic damage.

Between my junior and senior years, I had a choice between doing a rotation on dermatology or being an medical service intern for the summer at San Francisco General Hospital. One of the best decisions I ever made in medicine was to choose the internship.

During this 2 month rotation as an intern at San Francisco County hospital I learned a great deal about patient care. What I learned on this voluntary rotation stood me in good stead for the rest of my life. The grade I got on this elective rotation was instrumental in me getting a prestigious urology residency.

During our fourth year I was on a pulmonary medicine course rotation when our professor stopped at small child in the pediatric ICU. The child was on a respirator. When he told us the child had a persistently high Pco2 while on the respirator. He asked us how we would correct this problem. Two or three of us gave their answers. The answers were mostly dealing with the settings on the respirator. When he got to me I said I would correct the problem with a pair of scissors. The other students looked at me sort or strangely. He said to me, "You get an A in the course". The fact was that the expiratory tube from the respirator was too long to allow for the proper clearance of co2. I may not have made that answer if I had not taken that elective at San Francisco

County Hospital (now named Zuckerberg San Francisco County Hospital).

There was a student in our dormitory from Nepal. He chewed betel nut and his teeth were completely black. Once the dental hygienist students saw him he didn't have a chance. They took him to their lab and used him as a guinea pig to train several students during that year. When they were finished with him he had perfect white teeth. He couldn't stand it and went back to chewing betel nut.

I joined the Phi Chi medical fraternity and met my wife at a party there over a pool table. She was beautiful and extremely intelligent. We had two great children.

Some of our more creative students made a class movie at the end of our four years. It typified our class and was very provocative and funny. The movie opened showing a few of our classmates dancing with a nude dancer from the North Beach area of San Francisco. It showed some of our classmates picking up one of our Medicine Department professors in an ambulance down on the skid row section of San Francisco. Another segment showed a UCSF neurosurgeon doing brain surgery with a sandwich and a can of beer hanging from brace around his head and wearing a Foley catheter in order to survive another 12 hour surgery. In still another segment, the Chief of Surgery, and recent past president of the American College of Surgeons, was seen digging up a body from the VA Memorial Cemetery to use as a cadaver because the department of was running out of donated bodies in the surgery lab.

The fact that these very prominent people were willing to do these skits with us meant to me that maybe they weren't as anxious to get rid of us as we thought they were.

Believe it or not we found time to learn a great deal of medicine in those four years. We were so fortunate to be exposed to this outstanding group of professors. I consider this medical school to be the best in the United States at that time. The education we received there would be with us for the rest of our lives. I feel so privileged to have been able to join this group of people for this exquisite journey through medical school.

CHAPTER 6

THE TUMULTUOUS 60'S

These years of our time at medical school and the next few years were to be monumental in the history of the United States. A major social revolution was taking place among the young people of the country. Demonstrations and confrontations were taking place throughout the country between those for dramatic social changes (many of the young people in our country) and those who were for maintaining the status quo. The Vietnam War was to reach its height during these years. Students were accidently killed at Kent State while demonstrating against that war.

Racial civil rights issues were being acted out throughout the country. The Watts Riot happened in the summer of 1965. Other riots followed. Two of our prominent leaders (Dr. Martin Luther King and Robert Kennedy) would be assassinated in1968. The Tet offensive in the Vietnam War occurred early in 1968. The Democratic National Convention in Chicago mirrored these divisive issues in the country and was the site of violent confrontations between demonstrators and police in the fall of 1968. 1968 would become a year of tremendous significance in the history of our country.

I was going to be intimately involved with two of these major events of that period of our country's history.

Chapter 7

Internship At Los Angeles County Hospital

Having gone to a very academic medical school, I decided to apply to Los Angeles County Hospital for an internship. My idea was to get some practical experience. Man, was that an understatement. This hospital was one of the largest receiving hospitals in the country. The others included Cook County Hospital in Chicago, Detroit Receiving Hospital in Detroit, and Bellevue Hospital in New York.

I started on the OB-Gyn service. I had delivered one baby in medical school. Actually, I caught it in my gown like a fair catch in football. Fortunately, I didn't fumble it. They're really slippery little things. In baseball we use to rub our hands in dirt to keep our bat from slipping in our hands. Unfortunately there wasn't any dirt in the delivery room.

By the end of the first night on the OB service at L. A. County Hospital I had delivered 4 to 6 more babies. We were only allowed to deliver babies to mothers who had had previous uncomplicated deliveries. There sure were a lot of those around!!

One thing about these multip (multiple births) mothers, they could deliver those babies in a hurry on some occasions. We delivered babies in bed, on bed pans, on gurneys, transferring from gurneys to delivery tables and finally on delivery tables. When those little guys and gals want to head for daylight there is little you can do to stop them. You learn early on to roll with the punches.

Fortunately, we had excellent supervision by the residents and attending staff. These very competent doctors did the primary and complicated deliveries.

One of our intern partners was late in arriving to the hospital. She had been delayed in arriving because of family issues. By that time, we had enough experience to advise her on certain procedures. She wanted to go into Ob-GYN. She was anxious to learn how to do a caudal anesthesia on these mothers. We tried to tell her that may not be necessary on all of these patients. I remember watching her do a caudal block on one of these patients. The patient was on her side. Our intern partner was really was concentrating on doing that caudal block when someone said, "Ah, it's about the baby, its half way out!" After she got over the shock of hearing that she recovered nicely to finish the delivery.

Many of these mothers did not stay in the hospital for long. Some simply picked up their baby and left. It was sort of like an In and Out baby delivery service.

All in all, we had a great experience with these mothers. They were happy women. There were a few times when our experiences with them became funny or even hilarious.

It was a time just after birth control pills had come out. In the beginning, there was some confusion among all women in the country on how to use them. This confusion lead to some interesting situations in the OB-GYN clinics of LA County Hospital where we were working.

One lady came in pregnant. I asked her if she had taken the birth control pills as instructed. She told me she thought you were supposed to give them to your husband!!! Sorry about that lady, but they don't work that way.

Another pregnant lady told me she used them like aspirin. Every time she had sex she took one!!! I think she ran out of pills before the month was over.

The final case of this error in understanding of how to take the pills took the cake. It occurred when I was examining a pregnant lady in the clinic. I noticed that she had these little spots in her vagina. You guessed it. She had put those pills where she thought they would do the most good!!! I know this sounds like a skit on Saturday Night Live. You had to be there to appreciate it.

My next intern rotation was on the Urology service. I had been looking forward to this because of my interest in Urology. Guess what. The Los Angeles Watt's riots of 1965 started shortly after I arrived on Urology. This was to be a major historical event in the Civil Rights struggle of our country.

The riots started spontaneously and there was no warning that a riot was about to start. It was a hot summer Friday night in August. Apparently, there was an altercation between the police and black man in Watts (a black neighborhood in south Los Angeles). This incident exploded into a full-scale riot. Rioters were attacking police and police ware attacking rioters. Watts was ablaze. There was looting everywhere. The wounded rioters and some first responders were sent to Los Angeles County hospital where unsuspecting interns and residents were working.

There was a policy in effect at the hospital that channeled patients under police custody to the 13th floor where there was a "jail ward". One intern was working on this ward. On this night, a good friend of mine and a fellow UCSF medical school classmate was working on this ward. Within minutes 3 or 4 major gunshot wounds descended on him. They had by-passed the emergency room and had come to the 13th floor ward as per policy. He thought World War III had just started. He called for help. "Any surgeon to the jail ward STAT" came over the intercom. We all ran up there to find three or four patients with major gunshot wounds lying around the ward. One patient had a "sucking chest wound" and was in immediate need of a chest tube in addition to further surgery. I'll never forget that scene when we got to that ward.

These patients were immediately transferred to the surgery receiving ward. They all required surgery. All further such patients were directed directly to the surgery receiving ward. Once it was realized what was happening all the surgical teams were called in.

Watts was burning in many places. Rioters were being wounded and killed. Initial responders were being wounded and killed. To make a long story short, there were 34 deaths and over 1000 people wounded or injured over a five-day period.

The National Guard was called into the Watts area. They were ordered to shoot to kill if necessary. Unbelievably, a future good friend of mine and fellow urologist in San Diego for many years was the doctor assigned to the National Guard unit sent to the city (another unique coincident). He and his medical unit personnel were ordered to defend themselves with their guns if necessary. They received wounded National Guard soldiers into their medical unit.

A rioter tried to run a National Guard barricade with her car. The car had "Molotov cocktails" in the trunk. They stopped the car with a machine gun. The driver was taken to "the Big County" (another name for L. A. county hospital). She could not be saved.

When these wounded rioters arrived at the hospital they still were very mad. It wasn't uncommon for them to threaten to kill us when they got the chance. They eventually cooled down after they realized how hard we were working to help them.

As a urology intern one of my jobs was to do kidney x-rays on the patients to determine if they had a kidney injury. My most vivid memory of this was seeing the leg irons hanging off the patients' feet as I was doing their x-rays. I was amazed how many times you could be shot and still be fighting mad.

Nearly all of these gunshot wounds needed surgery. There were seven operating teams available and all were called into action. The operating rooms were going day and night. One of my fraternity brothers from our undergraduate days at UCLA was heading up one of the teams. As I recall about 90 gunshot patients were treated on Friday and Saturday nights alone. Martin Luther King came to the city to address the people of Los Angeles. He tried in vain to help stop the riots.

Many of the surgical procedures done in the hospital were complicated and the some of the patients required repeat surgeries. A lot of these patients required long stays in the hospital before their surgical problems were resolved. This was truly a combat experience. Many of these surgeons and other doctors caring for these patients would see actual combat in Vietnam in the next few years. All the ancillary services such as the blood bank and the laboratory service were going full speed ahead

A quarantine was instituted in Watts. Many of the nurses who lived there could not get to work. Available nurses worked double shifts. Volunteers came in to help provide basic nursing assistance. Many of these volunteers were the doctor's wives. As time went on we became friends with the rioters. We shared many good stories and jokes with them.

I remember one post-operative patient would tell us we were working too hard and we should take a break and sit down by his bed and watch some TV with him. He had a brand new TV on his food stand.

I can tell you one thing, this same guy was some sort of important dude in his community. When he finished his meal, he would snap his fingers and another patient on the same ward would get out of bed, struggle over to this guy's bed dragging his IV's behind him and buss his tray. Are you kidding me? This guy was surely some sort of powerful person.

All of the patients from the riot who survived were eventually discharged from the hospital.

The busiest day I had that year was on the orthopedic service when a resident, another intern and I admitted 20 patients and did 6 surgeries in one 24 hour period of time. There were two floors of diabetic patients on the Internal Medicine service. Another hospital next to the Big County was devoted solely to pediatric patients. The Infectious Disease service had its own separate location. We used non-disposable metal needles for IV infusion of blood and fluids. Plastic interact needles had not been developed yet. Butterfly needles were just starting to be used in pediatric patients.

When I rotated onto the General Surgery service my team had Friday night as our admitting night. We were on call for the "Knife and Gun Club" of Los Angeles. Knife and gunshot wounds frequently occurred on Friday nights in Los Angeles, not to mention the occasional riot. There seemed to be an endless line of surgical patients needing admission to the hospital. Most of these would need some type of surgery during their stay in the hospital. In addition to these patients there were those who were having elective surgeries. This was a very busy service.

It would be impossible to tell you about all of these patients, but a couple stood out. One patient we admitted had a history of being shot in the butt as he was climbing out the window of his girlfriend's bedroom. In this case she happened to be married to someone else.

Because this wound severed his lower spinal cord he became paraplegic. Over the years he developed severe pressure ulcers in the area of his rectum. He also developed recurrent life-threatening infections resulting from local infections in this area. He eventually required a hemi-corpectomy in which the lower part of his body would be removed. This an extremely complicated operation where the patient's lower body is removed below the waist and pelvic area. Separate diversions were made for the gastrointestinal and urinary tracts. When the surgery is completed the patient could sit in a sac in a wheelchair. This heroic surgery was done to save the patient's life. The procedure worked well and he was able to get around in a wheelchair.

One especially interesting case occurred when a patient was admitted after he had been stabbed in the lower neck. The stab wound was at the base of his neck on the left side, just above the collar bone. This is not a good place to be stabbed (not that there is a good place to be stabbed). There are many vital structures in this area. There are major arteries and veins located there. There are sympathetic and parasympathetic nerves there. The thoracic duct empties into the large venous system right in this area.

The thoracic duct is a delicate tubular structure that collects a fatty nutritious fluid (chyle), which has been absorbed from the gastrointestinal tract and transports this milky fluid to the point where it is deposited into the major venous system. Once the chyle reaches the venous system it is distributed around the body to various fat storage areas where it can provide energy needs for the body. As noted, this site of the emptying of chyle into the venous system is right where the stab wound was in this patient. His thoracic duct was lacerated and the chyle was leaking into the left chest cavity.

Fortunately, the bleeding in this patient was self-limited and stopped on its own. With an injury to sympathetic nerves at the base of the neck you can develop Horner's Syndrone. This syndrome results in ptosis (drooping eyelid), miosis (small pupil) and anhydrosis (dryness of that side of the face). The patient had all of these findings.

Because of the problems with his thoracic duct injury he was in the hospital for a long time and we made rounds on him at least once a day. Soon he was able to recite his own history and physical findings himself. When we were making rounds with our attending staff he would say, "I was stabbed in the neck right here, pointing to the stab wound, and ended up with Horner's syndrome, which means I got a small pupil, a droopy eyelid and dryness of my face, right here". To this day I can still hear his presentation of his own case and the resultant physical findings he had!

The laceration of his thoracic duct was a serious issue. When the thoracic duct is lacerated the chyle can drain into the left chest cavity producing a condition known as "chylothorax". This energy-rich fatty solution would now end up in his left chest cavity. This happened in our patient and the leaking chyle began to fill up his left chest cavity. We decided to drain it out of the chest cavity by needle puncture of the chest whenever the left chest began to fill up. The solution was then given back to him by mouth. This clearly wasn't a very good solution to the problem.

After one of these needle drainage procedures he developed a pneumothorax (collapsed lung). A chest tube was placed immediately. To our surprise the chyle began to drain out of the stab wound in his lower neck. Somehow the pneumothorax had sealed the leakage of chyle into the chest cavity and the leaking chyle ended up coming out of the site of the original stab wound. We put a sealant bag over the stab wound and began to collect the chyle in the bag. The bag began to fill up with this skim milk-like solution. Again, we gave the chyle back to him by mouth. Once again, this was not a very good solution to the problem.

We discussed what we could do next. To operate in this area and try to repair the duct would be impossible because of inflammation and scarring. All the experts were giving their opinion on what to do next. No one seemed to have a good solution.

One day, we were presenting the case to an older, very experienced downtown surgeon. He suggested we put "gum guaiac" into the stab wound to see if that would seal the leak. Gum guaiac is a sticky, brown gum-like material used in the old days to treat certain wound problems. How could something that simple work in this complicated problem?

The gum guaiac was applied. Low and behold the leakage stopped and no chylothorax recurred. Are you kidding me? This simple, old time remedy really worked!! We were overjoyed. We were very impressed with the value of this surgeon's experience. He definitely was our hero after that. The patient was eventually discharged from the hospital. We kind of missed having him around, but not enough to have that leakage of chyle start again!!

Believe it or not, I developed appendicitis the last night of my internship. The director of surgery asked me if I wasted to go to one of the major private Los Angeles Hospitals for my surgery. Man, they couldn't do it any better than the guys I had been working with. I decided to have the surgery done by the chief surgery resident I had been working with.

The only disadvantage was that when I was shaved and naked on the operating table several of the nurses came by and peered through the small window in the operating room door. A couple of them smiled and waved, which I thought was nice of them. Are you kidding!! How would you like to be lying there shaved and buck naked and have your co-workers stop by to say hi?

All in all, we interns had gained a tremendous amount of experience during our year at the Big County. We had been involved in one of the major historical event that would be part of the memorable and tumultuous years of the 60's in the history of the United States.

We were well trained in the care of trauma patients. Many of us were going to get a chance to use that training in the Vietnam War. At this time (1966) all interns and residents were being drafted to serve in Vietnam, except for those who joined the Military Reserve or were disabled in some way. I volunteered for the Navy and would be assigned to the Marine Corps.

Chapter 8

House Calls In Los Angeles

After my internship, I signed up with a group of doctors and would make emergency house calls for them in the Los Angeles area. This service was designed to improve patient care by attempting to bring care to the patient at times when they could not get to the doctor's office. Minor problems could be treated at home and more serious problems would be referred to the hospital. These were the days before Emergency Medical Response services with EMTs on board and intermediate care facilities (Urgent Care Centers) were available. The program was simply an attempt to treat patients outside the acute care centers.

All in all, this program did a lot of good work, but as you can imagine it was not an efficient use of time and resources. It was eventually discontinued in favor of some of the above noted programs. For me it was an interesting second job. On occasions, it became a real adventure full of plenty of excitement and, at times, humor. I'm will tell you of a few of the more interesting situations I encountered.

One of the first nights I was on call for this House Call service I got a call from downtown Los Angeles stating that there was a man in this apartment building who was trying to kill his wife with a fork. I tore down there in my old, chrome-less '57 Ford. Sure enough, there was a guy in this apartment, in the middle of Los Angeles, being held down by a few people from the building. He apparently had been chasing his wife around carrying a fork and threating to stab her. I gave him a shot of Thorazine. He eventually relaxed and we waited for an ambulance to arrive.

When I got back to my car a policeman was writing me up for double parking. I pleaded my case to no avail. Despite the fact that I told him that I was trying to keep someone from being killed with a fork, he continued to write the ticket. He sympathized with me, but said he couldn't tear the ticket up because it was already half done. He said I could explain these circumstances in a letter to the judge in the traffic court. Thanks a lot, man, see if I ever come down here again to save a lady from being stabbed with fork.

I got another daytime week-end call from East LA stating that a young pregnant girl had had a stroke. Fortunately, I had seen this problem before during my OB experience at the "Big County". There was an anti-nausea medication being used commonly that could produce a stroke-like physical deformity in the patient. This problem could be reversed easily with an IV injection of Benadryl.

I drove down this bumpy, dirt street in East LA looking for the address of this patient. Sure enough, when I get there, there is this young pregnant girl lying on the floor in a stroke-like position. I gave her the injection of Benadryl and she immediately got better.

While I'm accepting the gratitude of her mother, suddenly I hear a large crashing sound from outside the house. I'm thinking, "There goes my beautiful 57 Ford". After that, some crazy guy starts beating on the door. One of the kids gets up and locks the door. I'm beginning to look for another way out of this East LA house. The mother tells me not to worry. This guy is her ex-husband and he gets drunk and does this every so often. She says he'll get tired and go away. I'm still looking for a back door! I'm hoping that the guy isn't armed, and I don't mean with a fork. Sure enough, the beating on the front door stops and I hear a car drive away. When I look out the window I see my car is still there and it looks the same as it did when I arrived. I finish my paper work and left the house, much relieved that I'm still in one piece. Another boring day on the job---.

One weekend day I was sitting in a nice little restaurant in Altadena having lunch when I got a call stating that there was a lady in Los Angeles having chest pain. I jump into my car, flip a U-turn across 4 solid yellow lines and head for LA. You guessed it, I hear this siren behind me and a policeman pulls me over. He says, "Sir, do you realize what you just did?" I reply, "Yes sir. I'm Doctor Emery and I just received an emergency call from a woman in Los Angeles. She is having severe chest pain". He takes one look at me and my car and says, "Sir, I want to inform you that anything you say here can be used against you in a court of law". My reply, "Yes Sir, but I do have a card here with her number on it". He took the card and went back to his car. He seems to be there forever. I'm imagining him checking to see if I'm on America's ten most wanted list or my car is stolen or whatever. Pretty soon he comes up to my window and says, "Hey Doc, you want an escort to LA". I smile and say, "No thanks, Sir", and I speed away in that 57 Ford emergency vehicle.

One night I get a call from a downtown Los Angeles Hotel. Apparently, there was a sick patient in one of their rooms. When I get to the room there are three guys there dressed in suits or a white shirt and suit pants. One guy says, "Doc, Fred back there needs a sedative, he isn't acting right." I went into the bedroom and there was this guy lying on the bed fully dressed. He looked semi-comatose to me. I don't know if he was in a diabetic coma, had a drug overdose, had been poisoned or what. One thing I do know, he did not need is a sedative!!

Here I am in a back room of a hotel suite with a medical bag with full of drugs, in a situation that's looks like a scene out of the "Godfather". I go back in the main room and tell them Fred needs to go to the hospital. They want to know why I can't treat him there. I tell them again of my impression and urge them again to take him to the hospital. They thank me and escort me to the door. They give me the payment and a small tip (--- nice guys). All I could do is hope they followed my recommendation.

One might after midnight I got a call from southeast Los Angeles stating there was a sick baby in an apartment there. Remember, I am a young doctor trying to do a good job. Ok, I drive down there. Its dark and it's hard to read the street signs. Finally, I find this apartment. There are no lights on. I knock on the door and this heavy guy wearing a "wife beater" answers the door. "Who are you", he says. I know I'm not going to say what I'm thinking, "Who the hell do you think I am, a TV repairman". I, of course, choose a less confrontational course and say, "I'm Doctor Emery and I am here to see the sick baby". He told me that the baby had stopped crying. He got his Medi-Cal card out to have me bill it. Man, I couldn't believe it!! This guy called a doctor in the middle of the night because his baby was crying. This is another reason that this house call service was doomed for failure. Fortunately abuses of the system like this didn't occur often.

One of my more exciting events occurred when I was called to see a patient in a downtown motel. The patient was on the second floor. He was on the bed and complaining of chest pain. I was examining him when suddenly he had a cardiac arrest. I pulled him on the floor and began CPR. I asked his wife to call an ambulance. A guy walked by the window. I yelled for him to come in. I showed him how to do the percussion part of CPR. I continued to breathe for the patient. I told the ER at Big County what we were bringing him in. When the ambulance arrived, we put the patient onto a stretcher and into the ambulance without interrupting the CPR for a dangerous period of time. When we arrived at the ER the patient was alive and had a pulse. I don't think he survived after being treated in the hospital.

Chapter 9

The War In Vietnam

After these invaluable experiences in and around the Big County, I received orders to report for a physical examination (I guess you could call it that) before I was to report to my duty in the U.S. Navy Medical Corps assigned to the USMC. The physical exam I had could best be described as quite unusual. After I was drafted I took the physical exam with other inductees in Los Angeles.

Physical requirements for doctors were not too demanding. The examining medic would ask everyone to stand up and run in place. Then he said, "Sit down, Doc". Same thing happened when he asked us to do 10 pushups. Same thing happened when he asked us to stand on one leg. Finally, he asked me to come forward. He raised his hand and asked me how many hands he was holding up. I said, "One". He said, "Ok, Doc, you passed. Go get measured for fatigues."

It seemed to me, if you were a doctor and could see, walk (not too far) and talk, you were suitable for duty in the military. My doctor friends and I passed with flying colors.

There was a lottery mechanism in effect for drafted doctors. If you got the lottery you were allowed to finish your residency before you went in. I did not get the lottery and was assigned to The Third Marine Air Wing in El Toro, California. I was ordered to report there in March of 1967. I had eight months before I was to report for duty.

March came around and we headed for the El Toro Marine Air Station. My wife, our daughter and I would live in Tustin, which is a nice community close to El Toro. My first orders were to report to Camp Pulgus, which was a camp within Camp Pendelton (north of San Diego), for an induction into the Marine Corps.

At camp Las Pulgus I joined a group of professional officers consisting of doctors, dentists, lawyers, and chaplains. As a group of professionals, we were Navy Reserve Officers assigned to the Marine Corps. We moved into a small barracks near Camp Pulgus. An area of Camp Pulgus had been set up as a typical Vietnamese village and the surrounding area. We were given fatigue uniforms and began our induction course.

This induction course would give us a glimpse of the Marine Corp mission in Vietnam and what we could expect to see there. We began by attending lectures on the history of the USMC given by a staff sergeant. We learned about the history of the Corps from Tripoli to Korea. We were told of a famous statement made buy the Marine commanding officer leading a withdrawal from the Frozen Chosen reservoir in Korea. He was asked if he was retreating. His reply was, "Hell no, I'm fighting in reverse". We were going to learn that this attitude prevailed throughout the Corps. We were told how the Marines got the name "leather necks". Early in their history they provided protection for American ships who were being attacked by pirates. The pirates often tried to slash the Marine's necks with their swords. The Marines began to wear leather straps around their necks to protect this area from the pirate's swords.

We were told we were going into a combat zone and were asked what we were supposed to do if we were fired on by the enemy. Our responses varied. Some of us said we would hide behind a rock or look for a hole to jump in. One guy said he would hide behind another guy. We were all wrong. We were supposed to return fire and run at the enemy in a specific pattern. His opinion was that we would be harder to shoot if we ran towards them. I'm not sure if we all agreed with his reasoning. We would soon get the chance to demonstrate what he was talking about.

We were shown various types of equipment that was being used in Vietnam. One of us had his toe under the ramp of an APC when the ramp came down. He completed the course on crutches. We climbed rope ladders. We fired 45 pistols and M14 rifles.

We were shown many types of booby traps that the enemy was using against American soldiers. Many of these involved the use of punjie sticks. We were shown the types of road mines that were being used there. It was pointed out to us that the enemy could use almost any piece of US equipment, including a coke can, in the construction of a booby trap. The Marines left nothing behind on the battlefield.

We learned about the Ho Chi Minh trail. The main portion of this trail was in Cambodia, which was off limits to the American efforts to interrupt the trail. Many side trails extended into Vietnam. Massive amounts of material were brought down this trail by hand or on bicycles.

We learned about the extensive tunnel system that existed in the country. It was amazing that large troop concentrations, materials, and even hospitals could be located within this tunnel system. The hospitals were staffed with French trained doctors and medical personnel. The medical care delivered there was very good considering the circumstances.

We were told we were going to actually attack the enemy on a hill. We were given M14 rifles with blanks in the clips and attacked this hill there at Camp Pulgus in the manner our sergeant had told us to. Up the hill we went in a zig zag pattern firing as we went. Fortunately, the rattlesnakes had not come out yet in that Southern California desert.

Our big chance to demonstrate our ingenuity came when we were told we would be going on a night patrol and see what it was like to get ambushed by the enemy. One of our chaplains came up with a great idea. We would start out on the patrol as ordered. He would then lead us well off the trail. The Marines would think we were lost. When they came to find us we would ambush them. This chaplin (a Catholic priest) obviously missed his primary calling. He could have been a great guerrilla army leader.

The big night came and we set out on the patrol. Just as he had planned the Chaplin led us off into a remote part of the area. A half-hour or so later here they came. "Doctors, doctors, where are you?" When they got real close we let them have it!! We emptied our blank-containing magazines at them.

Those Marines thought that was the greatest thing that ever happened to them. They couldn't believe what a great joke this was. After that they did not hesitate to throw smoke bombs into our camp anytime of the day or night.

One thing we took away from that induction course was that those Marines were going to be ready to fight when they got there. They were going to demonstrate that to me later in Vietnam.

I returned to El Toro after our induction course was over. One night in the emergency room I was sewing up a laceration on the face of a drunk Marine. He apparently had gotten the cut in a fight somewhere in the area of El Toro. What happened next, I will never have an explanation for. His friends decided to extricate him from the emergency room. Into the ER operating room they came. The on-duty corpsmen were trying to stop them. I got under the table and was watching this melee between the corpsmen and the Marines. I had to come out from under the table because one of our corpsman had a Marine in a choke hold and I thought he was going to kill him. Soon the MPs arrived and got the situation under control. I never could figure that one out.

Chapter 10

Vietnam

In July I was ordered to March AFB for a flight to Okinawa. My wife and our daughter went to Seattle to live with her mother while I was in Vietnam. My wife was 5 months pregnant with our second child.

From March AFB we took a commercial jet to Guam were we refueled and then went on to Okinawa. As we were landing in Okinawa this Air Force sergeant began to have a grand mal seizure. I was tending to him. I instructed the pilot to call ahead to the Air Force Base and tell them we had a man on board who had a grand-mal seizure.

After we landed something very unique happened. An Air Force doctor came on board to take this patient to a medical facility. His name was John Barry. Believe it or not, he and I were to do our Urology residency together at the University of Oregon Medical School a few years later. We became lifelong friends. Now that is an unbelievable coincidence.

Our group of Marines and I were sent to Camp David where we were to stay until we flew to Vietnam. I toured

Naha city for a few days before our fight. This was a bustling city. The military bases there were very impressive.

We loaded into buses the night of our flight to Danang, South Vietnam. I got on the bus and took a seat near the rear of the bus. I heard a loud conversation outside and saw a USMC sergeant was accompanying a USMC Major to the bus. They were talking loudly and joking as they got on the bus. They may have stopped at a bar before they got to the bus. I prayed they wouldn't sit next to me. Believe it or not, the Major plopped down in the seat right next to me.

"First trip over, Captain?" he asked. "Yes Sir," I replied. "How long you been in the Corps, Captain?" he asked. "Four months, Sir," I answered. "Four months!!" he said loudly. "How in the hell did you make Captain in four months? It took me fifteen years to make Major!" He was a "mustang" Major and had come up through the enlisted ranks. "Actually Sir, I'm a Lieutenant in the Navy," I answered. "Well, how in the hell did you make Lieutenant in the Navy in four months, Lieutenant?" he asked. By this time this conversation was the only thing you could hear in this deathly silent bus full of young Marines. "Actually Sir, I'm a doctor and they made me a Lieutenant when I came in," I answered. "A doctor! No shit! How long you been a doctor?" he asked. This conversation was definitely not going in a good direction. You don't get your license in California until you finish your internship. "One year, Sir," I answered. He says, "Wait a minute. You been a doctor for one year, they made you a Navy Lieutenant and are sending you to Vietnam. No shit!" he exclaimed.

How am I going to tell this Major that I am a well-trained, mass casualty exposed doctor? "Well Sir, you're just going to have faith in the system." I answered. I think he accepted that answer. For the rest of the trip we discussed a variety of issues. At one point, he asked me how many Marines were on the bus and how many I thought would not come home. I said absolutely nothing. He gave me his projections. He eventually fell asleep. Thank God for small favors

We landed in Danang after dark. There was a light, spicy, sweet scent in the air. We were taken to a series of bunkers and were told to sleep in these bunkers. I couldn't find a space inside the bunker and slept on top of this sand bagged bunker. All night long there was intermittent muffled sound of artillery fire. I later learned this was out-going "H&I" (harassment and indigenous) fire. This type of fire was used to harass the enemy. I think it was then that I realized that I was in an active war zone.

Danang is a large, heavily populated port city on the eastern shore of South Vietnam south of the DMZ. There were large Marine and Air Force Air Bases there. There were US Marine and Korean Marine infantry headquarters there. At this time of the war the US Marines and Korean Marines were doing most of fighting in the northern part ("I Corp") of the country. China Beach was an "in country" R&R center located on the beach in Danang

The airways were very busy with air traffic. The Marines were flying A-4, F-4 and A-6 jet fighter bombers. The Air

Force was also using the F104 jet. Helicopters seemed to fill the skies. Hues and Chinooks were the most frequently seen helicopters. Small spotter planes also were seen frequently taking off and landing. C-130 transport aircraft seemed to be everywhere. Danang indeed was a huge Air Base for the Americans and their allies.

A WW11 era prop fighter (A-1) was being used for ground support of troops. These planes were flown by American and Vietnamese pilots. You could barely see their heads of the Vietnamese pilots in the cockpits of these large prop driven fighters. The scuttle butt was that they were sitting on telephone books in the cockpits.

There was a large Naval hospital in Danang. Medical care of the allied soldiers in Vietnam was excellent. There were several factors that contributed to this excellent care. The doctors, nurses, corpsman (and medics), and ancillary medical personnel were superbly trained. Many of them were trained in prestigious medical centers throughout the country.

These medical care personnel were exposed to the latest advancements in patient care based on the understanding of basic human physiology largely due to the effort of professors at UCSF in San Francisco. They were well versed in the functions of the ICU. This effort was led by Dr. Max Weil at the University of Southern California. Dr. Tom Shire at Parkland Hospital in Dallas Texas (where President Kennedy was taken after he was shot) described the "shock lung syndrome" with findings taken from wounded soldiers in the war. This information would be used forever in medicine. The latest medical equipment was available to these people. Surgeons of all surgical specialties were available to the wounded soldiers. If these specialty surgeons were not available on site in the land-based hospitals, they were available on large hospital ships (the Sanctuary and the Repose) stationed off shore and easily reachable by helicopter.

This was a guerrilla war, which meant that there was no movement of front lines. With a few exceptions, the hospitals were stationery throughout the war. Well established procedures and patient flow patterns could be developed and perfected in these hospitals. This meant that the incoming wounded soldier would be treated as well as in any trauma hospital located in the United States. He or she knew if they got to the hospital alive they had an excellent chance of surviving. The survival rate among these wounded soldiers was higher than ever seen to that point in the history of American medicine.

The medivac helicopters saved countless lives in the Vietnam War

The greatest advantage the wounded soldier had available to him was the superb ambulance service in this war. Nowhere in the world could an injured patient get to a hospital as fast as they could in Vietnam. Courageous medivac helicopter pilots and their crews would risk their lives to get to the injured soldier to the hospital. Once a secure "LZ" (landing zone) was established a medivac helicopter would be there to pick you up. The speed of this patient pick-up and transport to the hospital could be many times faster than one would see in any medically advanced country.

After arriving at the hospital, swift and efficient treatment would be given. As soon as the patient was stable following their initial treatment, which nearly always included some type of surgery, the patient was medivacked to an intermediate care facility for recuperation or further surgery if necessary. These intermediate hospitals were military hospitals located in Okinawa, the Philippines and other places in the Pacific region. The patients were then transferred to a military hospital in the United States to complete their recovery. This smooth and well-coordinated evacuation process was another factor that contributed to the high salvage rate seen with these patients. God help you, if you went in the hospital for laryngitis, you'd probably have surgery.

I was certainly well trained and thought I should be involved in this hospital-oriented treatment of our soldiers. As many of you know, there are times in the military when you are given a duty station where you think you might not be best utilized. In retrospect, the medical care program I was to be involved in turned out to be an important part of our effort in Vietnam.

General Kulak was the commanding officer of all the Marines in the Pacific, including Vietnam. He had a great interest in a pacification program that was directed toward the Vietnamese civilians. Part of this program was to provide basic medical care to these civilians. As it would turn out, this is the type of medical care I would be involved with during my year in Vietnam. I as determined to do this job to the best of my ability. I was assigned to the 2nd LAAM Battalion at the First Marine Air Wing Air Base located in Chu Lai, Vietnam, which was on the coast some 50 miles south of the city of Danang in the northern part of South Vietnam.

Our company headquarters was located on the beach east of the large Marine Air Base at Chu Lai. The First Marine Air Wing occupied the air base at Chu Lai. It was the third largest American air base in South Vietnam, behind Tan Son Nhut air base in the southern part of South Vietnam and the Danang air base in the northern part of South Vietnam (50 miles north of Chu Lai).

There were numerous other naval and army installations in Chu Lai, including the Army Americal Division (First Air Calvary, 101 Airborne, 72nd Airborne and numerous other US Army units). Other units included a Sea Bee battalion adjacent to our battalion, a US Navy shallow water landing area and the 1st Hospital Company.

There also was a small South Korean Marine base there. These soldiers were referred to as the "ROK (Republic of Korea) Marines". These Marines would be some of the best soldiers in the war.

The responsibility of this large base was to provide air support and medivac missions for that part of South Vietnam, to conduct combat missions in that area, to provide medical care for the allied soldiers in that area and to receive supplies at the naval landing area.

Our battalion aid station was responsible for the outpatient care and some minor surgery for the Marines in our LAAM (light antiaircraft missile) battalion. Our second effort was to participate in the Vietnamese pacification program, known as MED CAP program. This program had been started by our battalion medical unit the year before I arrived under the direction of Dr. Kidd. We provided medical care for the civilians of Ky Hoa island. This island was a few hundred yards off shore across from the Naval landing beach at the north end of the Chu Lai area. There were 5 Vietnamese villages and one North Vietnam relocation village on the island. This relocation village was in a poor location and was much more primitive than the beautiful and well kept civilian villages there.

We loaded our medical supplies into a small trailer and crossed the water on a ferry to reach the island. We would visit each of the villages once a week. We provided very basic outpatient care for the civilians there. More serious problems were treated at their district hospital or, occasionally, at our 1st Hospital company. The civilians on the island were fishermen for the most part.

The Vietcong combat units had easy access to the island and attacked areas of the island three times during the year that I was there. There well may have some Vietcong civilian volunteers on the island. Our battalion had one missile battery unit on the island.

It didn't take me long to demonstrate my unfamiliarity with military protocol. One of my duties was to be the sanitation officer for our battalion. I would make rounds once a mouth, or more often if needed, and inspect our area looking for problems that would detract from our sanitation safety. On my first sanitation run the sergeant and I came across a one-hole outhouse near the c/o's office. I looked inside and saw a hole full of bodily waste products.

I asked the sergeant what it was and he responded, "That the c/o's shitter sir". "Shitter" was the name used for all the toilet facilities seen in the permeant camps. Usually these were a three-hole enclosed out houses. Half fuel drums were placed under the holes. These drums were pulled out periodically and the contents were burned with jet fuel. Obviously, there was a distinctive odor around these facilities. One of the least favorite duties of the enlisted men was to be on a shit burning crew.

One of the benefits of being the c/o was you have your own personal shitter. Unfortunately, in this particular case, there was just a hole dug into the ground under a small wooden out house. I asked the sergeant how long that shitter had been there. He said, "Since 1965, I think". I said, "Ok, I think I better condemn this one and make him a new one that complies with regulations". It sounded good, even if I did not know what the hell regulations I was talking about. He said he would do it right away.

At the end of our rounds I decided to go by the c/o's office and give him the good news. I said, "Sir, I'm happy to let you know that I have condemned your shitter and we are making you a new one". He said in a loud voice, "You what?" That wasn't the response I was hoping for. "I love that shitter", he said. "Sir, your shitter was a health hazard. You're new one will be much better", I replied. He didn't care, he liked the old one. His new shitter was in a nice little grove of two or three trees. It was clean and had a nice view from outside. The oil drum could be moved easily in and out. The smoke from the burning shit blew away from the house. It seemed to be an ideal place to relieve yourself considering we were in a war zone. Of course, he hated it. He didn't hesitate to remind me of my poor judgement every time he saw me.

Things didn't get any better when, one day at lunch, he asked me what would happen if he ate this bug on his fork. I think he expected some sophisticated answer of what would happen to his body after the bug was digested in his stomach. He didn't even smile when I answered, "The bug would die, Sir". I knew we were becoming friends when I saw the look of disgust on his face. I wonder why they did not tell us about these sorts of situations during our induction lecture.

I arrived in July and the rocket attacks began in October. The enemy was being devastated by the aircraft used by the allies and attacked them when they could. The air bases were a favorite target for them. They were using 122mm rockets which were brought down from the north by hand. These rockets were not too accurate and were used more as area weapons. They were easy for the Vietcong to launch. They were hoping to destroy air planes and helicopters with these rockets. Some did not strike a solid object and could be found in the fields around the base after the attacks. On the first night of the Tet Offensive of 1968 one of these rockets hit our bomb dump. I will tell you about this later.

In this war the wounded soldiers were flown over these battalion aid stations on their way to the hospital. These aid stations had received the wounded soldiers in previous wars before the advent of the modern helicopter evacuation system. However, one night we did have to pick up one of our lieutenants, who had been wounded in the southern missile battery of our battalion. Unfortunately, the battery was south of where a recently arrived Army unit was temporally camped. It was a very dark night and we had to drive along the beach in front of this newly arrived Army unit. We decided to have one our corpsman walk in front of the jeep with the head lights on as we passed in front of that unit. I'll never forget how brave Andy was walking in front of the jeep with the lights shining on him. The corpsmen there were some of the best people I had ever met.

This is a group of corpsmen who were in our battalion aid station

Home sweet home

Everyone was living in large "hooches" with tin roofs. I lived in an old refrigerator unit next to the sickbay. Our bunker was right next to sickbay.

On weekends we played football and softball in one of the open spaces in the camp. One day one of our corpsman said there was a marine softball pitcher that no one could catch. Of course, I was dumb enough to say that that was impossible. Down to the make-shift softball diamond we went. I learned that this Marine was the second-best pitcher in the Marine Corps. I had caught some in baseball, but not in fast pitch softball. Still, he had to be catchable. They gave me a glove and I began to catch in the game. He threw a drop ball, a curve ball and a "riser". When he threw that riser, it jumped up a foot or so right before it got to the batter. I could not catch the ball. I simply didn't know where it went when I put the glove in front of the pitch. I couldn't believe it! Besides not being able to catch that pitch, no one could hit it either. We had a lot of fun as the sergeant tried to explain to us how you were supposed to catch or hit that pitch.

Roger Staubach had been stationed in Chu Lai as a US Navy Lieutenant the year before I got there. There was a field there where he practiced. It was called Staubach Stadium. He would become a Hall of Fame quarterback with the Dallas Cowboys.

I was determined to do all I could to be of assistance to our effort in this war. Our major effort in doing this was to run our MED CAP program. I never sent our corpsman to do this job when I was not with them. In our program we would go to the island each day of the week and run a morning clinic in one of the villages. We treated minor problems such as superficial infections, minor cuts and relatively minor injuries.

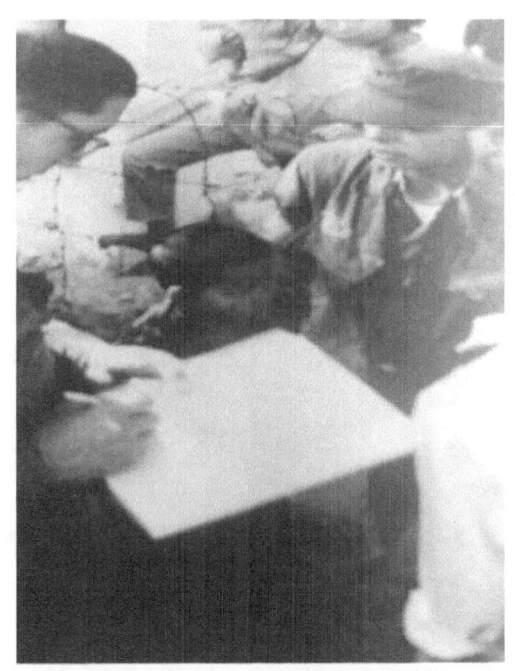

I saw some unusual ways to treat some medical conditions. One day we came upon the people treating a baby who had drowned. Their method of treatment was to make a fire and put their hands in it prior to rubbing the baby. To them this was a way to try to revive the baby by warming it up after it had turned cold.

Many of the people chewed betel nut. This nut provided some local anesthesia for mouth pain and it probably had some mild psychic effect on them. Eventually their teeth would turn completely black. We extracted some of these teeth with plyers when they were just sort of hanging there. We were just shortening the inevitable by a few days.

I saw one person who had developed muscle spasms from hyperventilation (inducing respiratory alkalosis and muscle spasms). They thought I was crazy when I had them breathe into a bag. They changed their mind quickly when the person got better.

There were local Vietnamese doctors around who were treating some of the sick civilians. I would talk to them through an interpreter. They carried vials of some antibiotics to inject patients with. They had a very strange solution in one vial. These vials carried a suspension of human placental extract in them. Their idea was that if the human placenta helped to provide nutrients to the baby during pregnancy, it surely would have some benefit to people when they were injected with it. Unfortunately, there is no medical basis for this thinking, but to them it seemed logical. To inject it could produce problems. Actually, I didn't see any problems from this treatment.

One day, after a Vietcong attack on the island I made a house call on a pig. The USAID program had sent Yorkshire hogs to South Vietnam as part of our pacification program. These hogs were prized processions of those who had them. This particular hog had been wounded during the attack. The people in the village asked if I could see the hog. Two corpsmen and I and a small Marine unit went to see this wounded hog. Fortunately, the hog only had a superficial wound of the abdomen. We cleaned the wound. I was so thankful the piece of shrapnel had not penetrated the abdomen. Can you just see me taking this Yorkshire hog into the First Hospital Company and asking them if they could do exploratory abdominal surgery on it!

During the war, our allied soldiers were accused of abusing some of the Vietnamese women. One day, on this island some Korean Marines were chasing some of the girls around one of the villages. Pretty soon a Korean sergeant showed up in a truck. He lined these soldiers up on their knees in front of everyone. He proceeded down the line giving each of them a powerful karate chop to the base of the neck. They fell over like a sack of potatoes. He then proceeded to do it for a second time. They then drug these soldiers into the truck and drove away. At least these soldiers were encouraged not to harass Vietnamese women.

The Korean soldiers had a great reputation as fighters. Most everyone did not want to cross their path. The civilians were afraid of them. We were afraid of them! One day, the c/o of the First Hospital Company asked me to take him to the island to see what we were doing there. I was glad to. He came out dressed in Korean Marine fatigues. The Korean soldiers had these large size fatigues made for him in appreciation for the care they had received at the hospital.

I suggested that he not wear those Korean fatigues to the island. I told him it might make the people think he was a giant Korean Marine. He thought that was nonsense and insisted on wearing those fatigues. He was very proud of them. During our tour of the island the Vietnamese kids all ran from him and the adults wouldn't even look at him. He did mention that he thought the people there were not very friendly. I didn't say anything. Other than that, I think he enjoyed the tour.

Later in the fall of 1967 the people of the central part of the island asked if we could help them with the construction of a small hospital-meeting house. We offered to provide them with the building materials. They would do the construction.

One of our best corpsmen, a Marine corporal and I loaded two 6-by trucks onto a private tug boat and began our trip to Danang. Once in Danang I went to the naval shipyard and spoke to the person managing that facility. I told him we were doing project as part of the US MED CAP program and needed some lumber to take back to Chu Lai. He told me that they did not have any lumber for such a project. I was extremely dejected when I told the others of the results of my request.

One of them said, "Don't worry, Doc. We can get the lumber. Go get a drink at the Stone Elephant Officers Club and we will call you when we're done. All we need is 20 bucks". I gave it to them and they disappeared with the trucks.

A few hours later they called me and came to pick me up. The two trucks were full of the lumber we needed. "How in the hell did you guys do that?", I asked with great joy. "We gave the fork lift driver a case of booze". No problem. We loaded the trucks onto the boat and headed for Chu Lai.

The men of the village constructed the building over several weeks. This building would serve as a small hospital and community meeting center. We had a dedication and celebration at the building. A great day was had by all.

A typical Vietnamese hospital bed. Note that the lower half is metal and has a drainage hole at the lower end of the metal plate.

That fall a US Army helicopter squadron decided to make their headquarters on the island. A construction unit came onto the island and began pulling up trees and clearing a landing zone for the choppers. The land and the trees were very valuable to the islanders. The choppers came in and tents were set up for the personnel of the unit. One night, shortly after that, the Vietcong attacked their area. They destroyed three or four of their helicopters. This Army helicopter unit left the island immediately after that.

The Vietnamese celebration of their new year is called "Tet". This celebration is the highlight of the year for the Vietnamese people. Families will often invite persons to their house who they think will set the tone in their family for the coming year. The corpsman and I had many friends on the island of Ky Hoa. We had been invited to some of their houses for Tet. Some of the corpsman and I decided to go to the island for the day of Tet.

That morning of Tet we got an intelligence report in our battalion headquarters that there were no active large units of the Vietcong in our area. The corpsman and I went to the island as planned.

I was visiting the nurse in the new hospital when she suddenly said, "VC, VC" and motioned for me to get under the bed. I got under the bed. The Vietcong were passing out leaflets in the village where we were. After what seemed like an eternity she said I could come out from under the bed. I didn't' know what these leaflets said, but it was a common way for the VC to communicate with the local population. They also tended to attack on holidays. This again was because of their poor communication system. If they used these holidays to base their attacks on, they could insure everybody was on the same page when they started the attack. The corpsman and I somehow got off the island safely. When I mentioned my experience on the Island, our intelligence officer didn't seem too concerned.

That night the whole damn place started to blow up. The attack started with a typical type of rocket attack. The big difference in this attack was one of the rockets hit the bomb dump. There were thousands of bombs in the dump. They all exploded at one time. We were over a slight hill 1/2 of a mile from the dump. Our camp lit up like many light bulbs going off in your face. The sound was deafening. Parts of the large hangers were knocked down. My friend on a hill above the air base thought we had been hit with a tactical nuclear weapon.

One of our flight surgeons was killed that night along with a pilot in the same bunker.

The Vietcong tried to breach the air base in several places. They were all killed. When we saw them on the ground the next day some of them were recognized as people who had been working on the base.

This Tet Offensive of 1968 was to be the largest battle of the war, as the Vietcong attacked many allied bases throughout South Vietnam. Some pockets or Vietcong resistance lasted for the next month. The city of Hue was one of these pockets of Vietcong resistance. Not only was this Tet Offensive of 1968 the biggest battle of the war, it was probably the turning point in the war when the American public began to question the reasons for us being there.

You could see from the Tet Offensive the Vietcong had unlimited and accurate information as to what the allies were doing. In contrast, the allies had almost no intelligence as to where they were or what they were planning to do. The enemy also could call up a fighting force on short notice. They seemingly only fought on their terms at the time that was right for them. This is what the allied forces were up against in this war. The enemy also had the advantage of living or hiding among civilians in "no fire zones". These no fire zones were set up by the US political and military leaders as places were the allied soldiers could not fire into. The decision as to where these zones where was probably made for political reasons. It wouldn't take the enemy long to learn where these zones where. Most of the enemy's concentrations were underground further making this war more difficult for the Americans and their allies.

Despite these huge disadvantages, the American soldier and his allies fought with great bravery and valor. They seemingly decided to fight the enemy on his terms. Fighting on the ground was done with small units. This meant that those in combat were usually young. These young enlisted men under the age of 25(the average of the combat soldier in the Vietnam War was 21) and officers under the age of 30-35 fought the enemy with great courage. Even today the American citizens are not aware or these facts.

Many of the people of our country blamed the soldiers for the war. Many of these soldiers were called "baby killers" when they returned to the United States. A large percentage of their contemporaries were so preoccupied with "anti-establishment" behavior that they had no idea of the fighting their friends had been involved in and the great courage they had shown while in the uniform of their country. They called them a bunch of drug addicts. Try going through the jungle looking for an invisible, lethal enemy when you are stoned! These attitudes of the country drove the soldiers from this war into a real band of brothers. Even today when they see each other they greet each other with the greeting, "Welcome home, brother".

These soldiers at the Vietnam Memorial look
exactly like the young men there.

These nurses at the Vietnam Memorial are comforting a wounded soldier. The nurses in Vietnam are forever ingrained in the minds and hearts of the soldiers who were there.

The year of 1968 became one of the most pivotal years in modern American history. In the winter we had the Tet Offensive of 1968. In the spring Martin Luther King was assassinated. In the summer Robert Kennedy was assassinated. In the fall there was the disruptive Democratic Convention was held in Chicago. This was truly a year of major events that would change our country forever.

There were some other factors in the Vietnam War which I think are worth mentioning. First, the soldiers, who went to Vietnam, went there one at a time alone. They did not go as part of a large unit. They did not have friends to talk to as they went. They did not know where they were going or what they would be doing when they got there. When they got there, they joined a unit of strangers. They were told not to make good friends because a person could be leaving soon or get killed before they got to know them. When they got there, they had 365 days left to serve "in country" before they would go home. The guy next to them might have 7 days left before he went home. He definitely was a "short timer". These circumstances had significant potential to create many psychological problems.

The older NCOs and older officers had grown up in the 40s and early 50s. They had a much different set of values and goals than the young troops and young officers, who were of the "baby boomer" generation. This might have placed them at odds with each other to a greater degree than could be explained simply by their age difference.

With regard to enemy POW camps in South Vietnam where they could hold Americans, I didn't think there were many because the enemy probably had nowhere to put a prisoner and could not afford to take care of them. I could be entirely wrong on that subject.

There were many other factors in this unconventional and controversial guerrilla war, which made it hard for the soldiers to explain the war to an American public, who had no frame of reference to understand anything they were saying when they came home. Basically, this war was between the American and allied forces against two separate enemy forces. One of the forces was the Vietcong guerrilla army and the other was the North Vietnamese army (NVA). The guerrilla army had many advantages. They were fighting in their country. They did not wear a uniform. Their objective was to terrorize South Vietnam civilians and to kill American and allied soldiers. They had exceptionally superb intelligence. The Vietcong would not fight the American and allied soldiers unless they had them greatly outnumbered. The enemy fighters were very brave and ferrous fighters and were willing to take heavy losses in order to obtain their objectives. They often attacked at night, giving them another advantage. Despite these advantages the American and allied soldiers fought them bravely and ferociously. I never heard any of them talking politics. They were simply carrying out the mission assigned to them.

Today, we in the United States are in another guerrilla war. A radical group of religious fanatics is terrorizing and killing Americans in our own country. Like the Vietcong, they are brave and ferocious fighters. They are willing to die to accomplish their objectives. Their task to accomplish these objectives is much easier than it was for the Vietcong in Vietnam. They are not fighting a well trained army, as the Vietcong were. They have freedom of movement throughout the country. This allows them to get at any target. They can infiltrate that target.

They, like the Vietcong, have superb intelligence. We have little or no intelligence about them. They can use a variety of simple weapons (a car, a truck, a bomb, a box cutter, an A-K 47, etc.) against Americans. Worst of all they know how to produce terror. They know that they will get much more terror out of bombing a day care center than they would by bombing an empty building. There is a tendency to call them cowardly thugs. We will have to learn more about them than that to be effective in fighting them. If we don't realize that they are well trained and dedicated fighters we will not have a lot of success in our effort to confront them.

This is a poster I made. I have given it to Vietnam veterans.
I plan to have it available at the Vietnam Memorial.

Chapter 11

Urology Residency At The University Of Oregon Medical School

A residency in the field of medicine can be viewed as a period of time when the doctor attends an intensive period of learning in a medical specialty. The residency can last from two to six or more years. The urology residency I attended lasted four years.

I did my Urology residency at the University of Oregon Medical School in Portland Oregon. The chief of this residency was Doctor Clarence Hodges. Doctor Hodges is very well known in the field of Urology. His papers on cancer of the prostate from the University of Chicago were monumental in the understanding of cancer of the prostate. Dr. Hodges and his professor of urology, Dr. Huggins, were awarded the Nobel Prize for medicine in 1941.

Dr. Clarence Hodges

Dr. Hodges was a very dedicated doctor. He was extremely intelligent and a true gentleman. He was a tremendous leader in the field of Urology and was respected by urologists throughout the world. His leadership style was unique in that he was not a critical person, but one who lead by example. He expected you to know when you made a mistake and be able to acknowledge it. His residents strived to approach problems as he would during this period of learning and for the rest of their lives. Many times, after I left this residency I would ask myself, "What would Dr. Hodges do when facing this problem".

My biggest surprise after I arrived for this residency was when I met Dr. John Barry. He was the same Dr. Barry I met in Okinawa when I was on my way to Vietnam (another one of the major coincidences of my life). I turned the care of a post-seizure Air Force sergeant over to him. We were to be co-residents for the next four years. We became very close friends. John went on to become the Chief of Urology at the University of Oregon Medical School. Dr. George Dechet was the third resident of our year. He is a tremendous person and doctor.

Equally surprising was the fact that Dr. Gary Van Gaulder was a resident in our program. Gary was the end on the Stanford football team in the late 50s. He was an outstanding offensive and defensive player. As I told you earlier, when I was a freshman at UCLA we ran Stanford's plays against the varsity in preparation for the upcoming Stanford game in 1957. I can specifically remember what the scouting report said about Gary. We became life-long friends after spending many hours together as urology residents in this residency. This was another major coincidence of my life.

Our children went to great schools south of Portland. The best Thanksgiving they had occurred when they were there. We had invited the family of John Barry over for the Thanksgiving celebration. That morning we put the frozen turkey on the back porch to thaw. Unfortunately, a local dog ate most of that large bird. The dog (or dogs) had eaten or carried off everything but the back bone and a few ribs. We decided that the remains would not provide much of a meal. We decided to go buy some hot dogs. Well, I'll tell you, those kids could not stop talking about how good that meal was. They kept insisting that that was the best Thanksgiving they had ever had.

The residency would last four years and would cover all aspects and surgical procedures of Urology including renal transplantation. Our first year consisted of general surgery and research. On general surgery, we rotated from surgical specialty to surgical specialty. We were involved with many routine and complex surgeries. My most flattering comment came when I was assisting the partner of Dr. Al Starr (well-known for the invention of the Starr-Edwards heart valve) in an open-heart surgery. I was holding a retractor near to where he was working. Suddenly he said, "Who's holding this retractor". I had a feeling he wasn't going to give me a compliment. I said, "I am". "What the hell do you think this is, a hemorrhoidectomy?" he responded. "No sir", I said. Oh well, such is the life of a junior resident.

The four years of this urology program involved hundreds of surgeries. For me to point out these to you would cause you to lose interest in this book quickly. For that reason, I have selected only a few examples of actual patient cases. Some of these cases had a tragic outcome. Bear in mind that the hundreds of other cases turned out well.

Dr. Hodges was a great inspiration to me. There were countless examples of this throughout my residency. He had a photographic memory. He could introduce you and your wife by your correct names a year after he had first met both of you. He knew the Urologic literature very well. He could refer you to specific pages of articles that pointed out a certain fact.

As for his own attitude toward patient care, he clearly was expecting us to do everything humanly possible to make sure that our patients got the best care possible. Our kidney transplant program was one of three in the United States. The other two were at UCLA and John Hopkins. Organ transplantation was in its infancy. The kidney was the first organ to be successfully transplanted. The first kidney transplant on the west coast was done at our institution two to three years before I arrived for my residency.

It was known that you had to immunosuppress the recipient of an organ transplant in order to improve the odds that the transplanted organ would not be rejected by the recipient patient. The basic immunosuppressive drug was Imuran. This powerful drug would suppress the immune system so strongly that the patient then could have the complications now seen with aids patients. Removal of the spleen of the recipient patient was also used to assist the immunosuppression. Prednisone was used as second immunosuppressive agent. Once the donor kidney was transplanted it was a matter of how strongly and for how long the rejection process of the recipient could be suppressed to allow the transplanted kidney to continue to function.

The usual scenario of the cadaver donated kidney transplant process was that the transplant team was notified that there were two kidneys to be available for transplantation. Two blood matched patients were then brought to our hospital and prepared for transplantation. Later that night they might undergo a bilateral nephrectomy (removal of both kidneys), a splenectomy, and a renal transplantation. One or two of us were sent out to the hospital where the donor patient was to do the bilateral nephrectomy on the donor patient.

At the time there was no good way to preserve these donor kidneys beyond a few hours. Because of this, the transplants were usually done at night. The availability of the donor kidneys was usually determined in the evening. The whole process required 4 to six surgeons to be available for the surgeries. The donor kidneys would usually arrive by 8pm to 9pm. The kidneys would be transplanted into the recipient patients. The recipient surgeries took up to three hours, especially if the recipient patient also needed a bilateral nephrectomy and splenectomy along with the kidney transplant. This meant that the transplant procedures could be completed in the early hours of the morning.

Live-donor transplant surgeries could be during the day on an elective basis. This was a much less complicated process logistically than the cadaver transplant process. It was simply a matter of transferring the donor kidney to the recipient patient.

The transplant ward consisted of recent transplant patients and patients who had developed complications after their initial transplantation. The complications that developed after a transplantation were varied and severe. At times, these complications were life threating. Under those circumstances the immunosuppression was stopped and the transplanted kidney was removed. If the removal of the kidney was delayed for too long the patient might die of one of the complications.

One point of this description of the transplantation processes is to point out another outstanding character trait of Dr. Hodges. One Saturday morning at our Urology rounds the resident on the transplant service announced that there were two cadaver kidneys that were going to be available later that day and he needed four volunteers for the procedures that day.

You can imagine that none of us jumped at the opportunity to do the surgeries, however we all raised our hands quickly in unison after Dr. Hodges raised his hand. He was quite serious about the fact that he was available to help. We all got a good inspirational lesson that Saturday morning.

When I was on the transplant service I spent many extra hours and days with the patients there. Apparently, Dr. Hodges thought I needed a break from my extended time on the service.

He got two tickets to the University of Oregon vs Stanford football game. He gave them to John Barry and asked him to take me to the game. The game was great. It was played in Eugene, Oregon. It featured two great college quarterbacks. Jim Plunket was the quarterback for Stanford and Dan Fouts was the quarterback for the University of Oregon. Both of these quarterbacks went on to have great careers in the NFL. It was a great game. Stanford won the game.

On one occasion, I was operating with Dr. Hodges as he was doing a transurethral resection of the prostate (commonly known as a "TURP"). This operation consisted of passing a operating instrument through the urethra and into the bladder. After that the bulk of the prostate was resected or electrically chipped out of the prostate gland. The procedure can accompanied by significant bleeding. To stop the bleeding you have to know a procedure to do that.

When I saw the amount of bleeding from this patient I said, "Dr. Hodges I don't think we will be able to stop this bleeding". He said, "I said the same thing when I was standing where you are and Dr. Foley was standing where I am". Was that the Dr. Foley whose name is on the most commonly used catheter in the history of medicine. Yes, it was. Then he said," Dr. Foley said to me, Clarence, put the catheter on traction (more pulling pressure) and let's go have a cigarette. If it's still bleeding when we are done with our cigarettes, were going have to look back in and stop the bleeding" When they returned from the cigarette break, the bleeding had stopped and the operation was over. The Foley catheter on traction would stop the venous bleeding. If that happened the operation is over. If the bleeding did not stop, then there was arterial bleeding still going on and we were going to have to look back in there and stop the arterial bleeding.

Did the cigarette smoking have anything to do with the story? Yes, it did. It takes 8-10 minutes to leisurely smoke a cigarette. It just so happens the human clotting time is about 8 minutes.

The nurses would tell me that they never had trouble with post-op bleeding from my patients, who had this operation. But they would be busy irrigating the blood out of the bladder of the patients who had had the same procedure by other urologists in that hospital. Later, when I was in private practice, I would try to explain this procedure urologists in my community.

A tragic incident was to occur on my rotation at the University Hospital. The cases that went to the University Hospital were the more difficult cases and cases that had been referred from the private physicians. This particular case involved a 17 year old young man who had exstrophy of the bladder. Exstrophy of the bladder is a congenital defect of the bladder in which the bladder did not close properly. The patient had been diapers his whole life. He was seen on my service and I elected to try to close the bladder. At surgery, I felt that the procedure likely would not work. Post-operatively he developed severe pulmonary problems and died despite all our efforts to overcome the problem. After he died he was found to have hypoplastic lungs. This was the cause of the lung failure. We had not suspected this preoperatively and had not evaluated his lungs completely. As a surgeon, you cannot ever forget this case.

Another tragic event occurred when I was on a pediatric rotation at Children's Hospital. We admitted a 11-year-old girl who had a ruptured kidney from a traumatic accident. In the past, these ruptured kidney cases were all operated on and the non-functioning parts of the kidney were removed.

At that time there was an alternate type of treatment being used to treat these ruptured kidney cases. The treatment consisted of not operating on these cases and observing them and allowing the kidney to heal itself. Many of these cases ended up with more functioning kidney tissue surviving than would have been the case if the patient had undergone surgery initially. We elected to treat the patient with this new method of treatment. Her course did not go well. She began to have bleeding and urine leakage in and around her kidney. This was expected to happen while observing her. However, we ended up watching her for too long. By the time we decided to operate on her she had developed severe heart and lung complications. She passed away after the surgery. These are the cases you carry with you for the rest of your life.

We did many surgical cases as residents. To go through these cases would be very boring for you. Instead of that I am going to tell you of some of the unusual experiences I had during those years.

Have you ever run bobcats in the mountains of Oregon in the winter? One of our residents, Rusby, loved to run hounds in the mountains around Mount Hood near Portland. His best dog was a little female hound he had bought from a friend. She had actually been burned in a previous accident. He had skin grafted her in the dog lab to help save her life. She was one of his favorite dogs.

The story of how he came to buy her from a friend was interesting. His friend had several good hounds and loved to run his dogs in the mountains around Portland. This friend called him one time and told him that he and his wife were struggling in their marriage. Finally, his wife apparently told him, "It's me or the dogs". He had to sell the dog to save his marriage.

A few months later his friend called him and asked if he could buy the dog back. Apparently, negotiations had broken down between he and his wife. He had changed his plans and decided to go with the dogs instead of his wife. Friend or not, he was not about to get that dog back from our fellow resident.

One day, Rusby asked me if I could meet in Lake Oswego and we could run hounds on Mt. Hood. We finally got up on Mount Hood sometime later. We looked for some bobcat tracks in the snow. Unfortunately, we didn't find any bobcat tracks. We did, however, make it back in time for our 7:00 AM surgeries.

I worked in a local emergency room to supplement our income. Here in Oregon the guys seemed to break bar stools over each other's heads, rather than stabbing or shooting each other. This resulted in a slightly higher survival rate than in Los Angeles. There still were plenty of things happening to keep you busy in the emergency rooms.

The Deschutes river runs south to north in central Oregon. My close friend and I were on the same service at the VA Hospital. I asked him if he would like to go fishing on the Deschutes River. Tom was from New York City and always talked about the bars on the windows there. I wanted to show him this river.

We got to the river for our fishing experience. He was in awe of the beautiful scenery. This time of year, the big trout were out near the banks catching the big mayflies falling off the trees. I'm talking big native trout. The river is pretty fast in that part of the valley. We waded in in our tennis shoes and shorts. As it turned out, I'm glad we could not afford waders.

I had no aspirations of catching a fish. I had much less hope for my city friend to catch anything. Suddenly heard a blood curdling scream from his position on the river. There was my friend out there in knee deep water staggering and jumping around with one of these 3 to 4 pound native trout on his line.

Dumb me! I forgot to ask him if he knew how to swim. I thought he would fall and be swept down the river. Thank God, we couldn't afford to buy waders. You fall, the waders fill up with water and you have a real problem. He didn't seem to be worried as he danced around screaming out there in that dangerous river like he had just won the Nobel Prize. I don't know how he did it, but he finally got that thing landed. It was a beautiful big native rainbow trout.

Meanwhile I was nervous wreck. I was trying to figure out how to tell his wife how he had drowned in this famous beautiful river. All I could think of was the prospect of dragging this beautiful river trying to find her husband. Thank God, he survived. Well, you would think my good friend from New York City had just landed Moby Dick. He couldn't stop talking about it. It was a great day.

I had another unique experience on another fishing trip. It seemed that I had many unique experiences while fishing. One of our residents had a small cement cruiser. He used it to fish in the ocean. You ever heard of a cement boat? My friend began to explain about water displacement as compared to composition of the boat, etc. He convinced us things were fine. Unfortunately, he did not mention anything about the motor. I should have known to stay away from a boat made out of cement.

One day, he asked two of us if we wanted to go "over the bar" to fish for salmon at the mouth of the Columbia River near Astoria, Oregon. I thought he meant we were going to a bar for a beer before we cast off from Astoria. Boy, was I wrong.

Ok, we cast off from Astoria in this small cement cruiser. You ever been "over the bar" at the mouth of the Colombia River. It's actually scary to terrifying. There is a sand bar out there in the mouth of the river. When you go over that sand bar the waves get very large. There you are cruising along and suddenly you are in these large waves. Right away I began to pray that cement boat wouldn't sink. The next worse thing happened. The motor quits!

Here we are in the middle of the mouth of the Columbia River and the motor quits!! Our fellow resident assures us that is no problem. Maybe he was use to the motor quitting. He couldn't' get the motor restarted. He was an experienced boater and handed the situation very well. He radioed the Coast Guard and asked them to come and get us.

You do realize that when you radio the Coast Guard for help, it's not like you called a cab to pick you up. They probably have a few other lives to save before they get to you. We waited and waited. More prayers that we don't sink. Finally, they got there and towed us back to Astoria. If I ever hear a person use the words cement and boat in the same sentence I will disappear in a hurry.

On one special occasion my wife and I went to the Salashan, a beautiful resort on the coast, for a few days. Sort of a second honeymoon. On the second day, she slept in and I decided to play golf.

I went up to the starter and he asked me if I could join the twosome on the 1st tee. I said, "Sure". He then told me that the twosome was Governor Mc Call and his wife. Thank God, he told me. I would not have recognized him. Man are you kidding, I'm going to play golf with the governor of Oregon and his wife.

I went up to him and said, "Good morning Governor Mc Call, I'm John Emery". He introduced himself and his wife. I told him what a pleasure it was to play with he and his wife.

They had their dog with them. Golf can be more causal in that part of Oregon. I played 9 holes with them. They were the most wonderful couple. I don't remember what we talked about. I was simply trying to give the impression that I was a semi-intelligent resident of the state.

Now I will tell you of one of the most unusual experiences I have ever had. My fellow resident and good friend asked me if I wanted to go on a fishing trip to Canada on the Dean River? The Dean River in British Columbia starts in a lake west of the Frazier River canyon in western British Columbia and flows 100 miles to the coast. You can only use flies while fishing on this river. At the start of the river there are 1-3 lb native trout in the river. At the mouth of the river there are 10-30 lb steelhead trout and salmon. The whole river is for fly fishing only. This area is a beautiful part of Canada.

My friend said there would be two school teachers going with us. One of teachers was a former basketball player from the University of Idaho. He also was from Portland. As I was to learn along the way, he had toured for Remington as an expert trick shot rifleman. He was a long axe throwing champion in Idaho. He was an expert skeet shooter. He was a knot tying expert. Man, I thought we were going fishing with a descendent of Davy Crocket or Daniel Boone.

We started from Portland in a Volkswagen bus. That thing hardly had enough horse power to get us partway up the Frazier River canyon. As we were going along, the Idaho long ax throwing campion school teacher asked me how much I would give him to shoot a nickel out of the air with a 22 rifle. I answered saying, "Ok, I'll give you 5 bucks if you do that" He says "How about two nickels". This is getting a little ridiculous. No one can do that. "Ok, 10 bucks", I answered. Quickest way I lost 10 bucks in my life.

We were driving through the forest of British Columbia in that underpowered bus when we stopped at a small isolated lodge-cafe on the unpaved road. As we were eating our last normal meal for a while, the subject of grizzly bears came up. An older gentleman who owned the café began to tell us of the prowess of this animal. First, he told us that they were coming out of hibernation this time of year (June) and were very hungry. He told us not to worry because they usually don't bother humans unless you disturb them with their cubs. I had seen plenty of black bears in West Virginia and California, but never a grizzly.

He said he had seen one carrying a cow down the road. Oh great, I'm glad he told us that one. He said they killed prey and then they put the prey on a pile with other prey and waited there to see if you stopped to check out the pile. If you did, you soon would be on the pile. Dude, I was getting more uncomfortable by the second. I didn't really like fish that much anyway. You can always buy a fish.

Then he proceeded to tell us how to kill a grizzly. They are the king of the forest and are very arrogant. Just when they get to you they stand up and growl loudly. At that point, you're supposed to shoot them in the neck with a 44-magnum pistol. I knew enough about anatomy to know what happened to the grizzly. He would be a dead quadriplegic bear. I began to make plans. I knew no one had a 44-magnum pistol with them and that didn't matter to me, because I wasn't going to get out of that VW bus anyway.

Then the owner of the café began to tell us of his skill as a pistol marksman. He said he could hit a tin can on a fence with a 44-magnum pistol at 30 yds. We finally had a comeback. Our teacher friend told him he could shoot a dime out of the air with a 22 rifle. That did it. The owner of the café said that was impossible. Out on the front porch we all went.

Our rifle expert teacher got the rifle. He threw the dime in the air. You could hear the "ping" when the bullet hit the dime. All of our jaws dropped, especially the guy who owned the café'. Our friend told him the dime came down about where you hit it. The owner got down on his hands and knees and felt around for the dime. He found it. We went back into the café. The owner got a card and wrote our friends name on it along with the story of how had hit the dime in the air with a 22 rifle. He had our friend sign the card. He nailed the dime and the card on the wall behind the bar. We left the café with the owner talking to himself. It was clear I was in for some kind of fishing trip.

We finally arrived at Lake Nimpo and rented two metal rowboats and a small motor and started across the lake. As you may have figured out, our friend had tied the boats together using these special knots. We finally reached the origin of the Dean River out of the lake. We started down the famous Dean River. The first part of the river meandered through a grassy and rocky valley. There were scattered Indian houses along the river. There were a few Indians along the bank. They were probably laughing at these four idiots with their tied together boats trying to negotiate this river.

We soon began to realize we were the only humans who were strong enough physically and mentally to reach our fishing destination and set up camp there. After what seemed like hours we reached a clearing on the north side of the river. We set up our camp.

The next day we got up and fished. It was unbelievable. My fingers were cut up from trying to get those large native rainbows off the hook. We obviously had fish for breakfast, lunch, and dinner. The next day and a lot of fish later the unbelievable happened! We looked across the river and there were four men dressed in their Ralph Lauren fishing outfits walking down the other side of the river carrying small suitcases. We thought we had just flipped out. What the hell were they doing in this remote place.

That night we waded across the river and met them. Turns out that these gentlemen had started out in Palm Springs, California. They flew to Vancouver, Canada and got a flight to Nimpo Lake in a sea plane. A guide then brought them by boat to a point not far from the cabin. They got out of the boat, picked up their suitcases and walked to a, what looked like, deserted cabin across the river.

Oh yes, the guide stayed on as a cook. Two of them were retired football coaches from the eastern part of the country.

The third gentleman owned a Cadillac agency in Green Bay, Wisconsin. His name was Don Hutson. He had a ring that read "NFL Hall of Fame – end".

Don played at Alabama, where he played with Bear Bryant, and was drafted by the Green Bay Packers. He and the Packers coach were largely responsible for revolutionizing the professional football passing game. Don asked me if I would take him down the river the next day and show him a good spot to fish.

The next day Don waded across the river. I took him to my favorite spot on the river to fish. The spot had a deep crevasse below a small waterfall. You could see the fish coming up to take the fly. I left Don there in that beautiful spot. That trip was one to remember forever.

To that date, I had not experienced any feelings or behavior that would indicate I had bipolar disorder. Of course, I knew very little about this disease at that time. Perhaps my drive to work extra hours was an indication I could develop some sort of accelerated activity level. I did make some bad social decisions.

Chapter 12

Private Practice

By the time I decided to start a private practice in Urology it was clear that I was a California citizen doctor. I had been a citizen of California since age 16. I graduated from Torrance high school. I attended UCLA as an undergraduate. I attended the University of California at San Francisco Medical School. I was an intern at Los Angeles County Hospital during the year of the 1965 Watts Riot. I was drafted out of the city of Torrance, California and served a year as a doctor in the war in Vietnam. I had jobs in Southern California with other citizens of California. I was proud of the fact that I was a citizen of California and sincerely believed that this state had given me the opportunity to become a doctor. I felt a strong a attachment to my fellow citizens of this state and considered it a privilege to be involved in their medical care.

After finishing my residency with Dr. Hodges, I decided to begin a urology practice in Southern California. I joined the practice of two very good urologists in July of 1973. My wife, our children and I were very happy to be living in that part of California. In addition to that we would be around some of her family who had come to California many years earlier. My dad's family had migrated to California from Canada in the early 40s' and we were to spend a lot of time with them.

I was sharing many patients and many surgeries with the two other doctors I was working with. They were both excellent urologists with each having added expertise in certain aspects of Urology. Fortunately, the practice began well. We practiced in two hospitals there. One was a large district hospital which years later joined with a large Hospital Corporation group. The other hospital was a smaller private hospital located to the west of the hospital described above. Occasionally we practiced in small private hospitals in that part of the county.

It was in this part of my life where I was to develop significant clinical findings of bipolar disorder. In retrospect, I think I had shown some subclinical findings of this disease before this time. In the early years of my practice I was very happy and things were going very well.

Those days were the days when the doctor and patient had a one to one relationship and doctors referred the patient to another doctor in whom he had confidence could help the patient. I was enjoying practicing with the two other urologists in our group.

Our children loved growing up there. They were good students and engaged in many extra curricular activities in their schools.

I was making many wonderful friends among my patients, the doctors of our area and the citizens of the city. I met the equipment manager of our local professional football team. I was able to get into the Chargers practice field occasionally which was a thrill for me. I also became very good friends with the professional football team doctor in our city. He was true example of a gentleman doctor. He was very well trained and was an excellent team physician. I was able to see some of the professional football players and coaches when they had a urologic problem.

In football, the most common urologic problem is blunt trauma to the kidney. This trauma can result in a myriad of injuries from a simple contusion, or bruise, to multiple fractures of the kidney. From the professional team I saw some kidney contusions and nothing more serious than that. Later in my practice I had a case of multiple fractures in a kidney from blunt trauma to that kidney in a college football player. I will describe this case later when I describe my cases of kidney fractures.

Early in my time in the city some friends of mine and I worked at the Andy Williams Golf Tournament. We worked in a small emergency medicine condo near the hotel during the tournament. We treated minor injuries in the condo and sent more serious injuries to the hospital. I was able to be in close contact with the players of the time. Some were treated in our facility for allergies and other minor problems. I met Andy Williams and his wife there. They were a wonderful couple. I developed a true love for golf which continues until this day. This was a wonderful job to have.

One of my early surgical cases was the removal of a very large kidney cancer in an elderly lady. This case was to be one of the most difficult such procedures I would do throughout my career. During the case a tear occurred in the vena cava, the large vein in the abdomen that returns blood from the lower body to the heart. I closed the tear quickly. I was use to sewing large veins together while doing kidney translations in our residency. This was one of the early realizations that I had had tremendous Urology training under the guidance of Dr. Hodges. I was extremely grateful for having trained with him. This gratitude continued for the next 40 years.

Were there any signs of bipolar disorder during these early years of practice? In retrospect, there may have been. At one point I suggested that we try to initiate a kidney transplant program in our part of the city. That idea was impractical. We certainly didn't have the facilities to carry such a program. Was this suggestion a sign of euphoria? Maybe. What do you think? Other than that there were no other events that suggested any sustained significant mood swing in my personality. That all changed after three years of practice.

Around that time something unusual happened. I began to worry about the post-operative course of a patient who was actually doing well. I continued to focus on that patient until it was clear I was having some inappropriate paranoia. It wasn't that I was imagining things, it was just that I was paranoid about this patient's post-operative course that was actually going well. In this particular case, my worrying seemed excessive and unfounded. I continued to focus on this unfounded worry. My partners and I agreed that I should take some time off and see if there was something wrong with me.

A short time after that I began my first major bipolar depression. After I took some time off I tried to exercise, but I couldn't. I began to get a feeling of total worthlessness. It seemed like the bottom had fallen out of my life. It got to the point that I considered suicide. I can assure you that this feeling was very painful, fearful and shocking to me. There was no bottom to this descent into depression. Then an unbelievable thing happened. Late one night I was truly thinking of suicide. At about 2 am my dad called and said, "John, don't hurt yourself". I was too sick to put the call into perspective. He did not know I was struggling with this depression. He had no way of knowing that I was considering hurting myself. This was truly the Grace of God at work. Truly, that call saved my life.

Shortly after that I simply decompensated into a deeply shocked patient. I fell to the ground and began to spontaneously cry out. My wife called a family member to help and I was taken to a hospital in the city.

If my lifelong friends had seen me at this time they probably would think I was on a horrible mental trip from a drug reaction. I'm not sure what medication I was given when I got to the hospital. I'm sure my case was a challenge for my doctor and the attendant health care professionals working on the ward.

Here was a high preforming doctor who was very ill from a major depression illness. I basically was in shock. When I woke up the next day I was very confused. I knew I was on a mental treatment ward but I wasn't sure which hospital I was in. This is an example of how this shock had disoriented me.

During this time, I was withdrawn into myself. I was ruminating on ideas that were destructive to my self-esteem. I was going over the courses of some of my patients. I thought I had done something wrong when these patients when actually had done very well. I was ruminating over all the things I thought I had done wrong during my life. The main thing for me while I was on this ward was to not draw any attention to myself while I was there.

On these wards you will be treated by your personal physician and his associates and you are also asked to attend group therapy meetings. Your personal physician will guide your psychiatric medical therapy. With regard to group therapy, you go to meetings during the day. The patients in the meetings have all types of diagnoses. In some of these meetings the staff encourages the patients to share their feelings and ideas with the other patients. If you've had a depressive illness you know that you don't usually share any experience with anyone, especially a group of people you don't even know. In cases of depression the patient is very guarded about sharing any information even with a family member or with a close friend. I usually made no comments in those meetings.

With depression diseases, the patient can become very malleable. This means that they can be guided easily into positions or places they might not go if they were well. For instance, I was encouraged to participate in a group workshop where we could work with our hands. I was encouraged to make a drawing or a figure out of pipe stems. Now, I felt even worse that I could not do that. This was a person who had done some of the most difficult surgeries in Urology.

If you have had a depressive illness, you know this illness can be physically painful. This is real pain. The most common feeling is a total loss of self-esteem. This feeling itself is psychologically painful. I also had was a feeling of tightness around my abdominal wall and my heart. This terrible feeling reached the point where it was constricting the flow of air into my lungs. These feelings are hard to describe to someone who has never had a severe depression. It's like trying to describe to someone how it feels to be run over by a car. Only those who have been there can understand what you are saying.

Interestingly, some the patients on the psychiatry ward can be of great help to you usually from a one to one conservation. "Hey, I know exactly how you feel" can be a comforting thing to hear when you are severely psychologically ill. I have met some great people on these wards.

When the conversation gets to the point where the other patient shares with you what worked for them to get out of these situations, it could be very helpful to you. This is not explained in the psychiatric journals or textbooks. The teaching there probably suggests that this might happen in the group meetings. In the acute hospital admission setting, this usually does not occur in these meetings, especially among those who are new to their illness.

I'm not suggesting that group therapy is not beneficial. Group therapy is extremely useful in all diseases. It's very nice to hear from other patients with the same illnesses that you have. These meetings are very beneficial to patients. What I'm saying is such meetings probably are not as beneficial to an acutely ill, unstable psychiatric patient. A one to one conversation with someone who has been where you are may be much more therapeutic to you. Such conservations are usually initiated privately by the patient who has been there before. As impractical and ridiculous as it sounds I might put up a sign in the psychiatric ward that said "We encourage you to see if you can help the person next to you".

As with other illnesses, time is an important factor in the recovery from an acute or severe swing of emotion like I have described as it happened to me. There were to be other similar episodes in my experience with this disease. Thankfully, I survived the first one. I could have easily succumbed from this illness during this first bipolar depression.

After I recovered from this depression I returned to work. No patient was affected adversely from my depression. As it turned out no patient would ever to be affected negatively because of my illness. I thank God for that.

Fortunately, I recovered all my faculties after this first depression episode. It seemed that the hole I had fallen through was repaired and I was back to myself again. There was no suggestion I had bipolar disorder as I established a relationship with a psychiatrist who was to follow me over the next five years with the diagnosis of one episode of depression.

As I mentioned in the introduction of this book, being at work can be important to you. I think you should return to your job as soon as you feel you can. Also in the introduction, I pointed out that I think you should try to get good at something so you can fall back on that skill to allow you to get back to that job when you feel you are ready. Today friends and colleagues of all of us seem to have much more understanding about this disease and are likely to help you get back to work.

When I returned to work I was slow to recover from the shock of the episode of depression I had experienced. I'm sure my open friendly personality was somewhat dampened during this recovery period. I tended to keep 100% of my focus on good patient care. I was so fortunate to not lose any of my knowledge of medicine or my surgical skills from this initial significant mood swing.

During those months and years I saw two or three different psychiatrists. The first one I saw was very understanding and began me on an antidepressant. We talked a lot about my past life and experiences. There was nothing in my background that would lead me to develop a depression disease. I had a wonderful family to grow up in. I had very cherished friends from my childhood in the mountains around the city of Charleston, West Virginia, and many friends I had in places I had been since then.

I talked to the doctor about our marriage. My wife and I had a tumultuous marriage. Our basic difficulty we had was the fact that I was a total day person and she was a total night person. She could stay up all night and frequently went grocery shopping late at night. I, on the other hand, was a total day time person. We were expected to be ready to start surgeries by 7:30 in the morning. I was a very structured person when I was working.

My wife's and my incompatibility was worsened by my disease. In some of my hyperactivity states later in the course of this disease I would leave the house and stay away for up to weeks. This was very hard on my wife. When I returned I became depressed and further damaged our relationship. For her part she wanted nothing to do with my illness. She said it was my problem and she wanted nothing to do with it. In retrospect, her attitude was the best for me. I had never been dependent on anyone since I left the home of my parents. I was to work my way through this disease myself.

We had the most wonderful children and both of us were very close to them. We spent long hours with them in their activities. We both loved them very much. Thank goodness, I did not say anything serious against my wife to them as they were growing up. The fact that I spent more than normal hours on my profession also took a lot away from our marital relationship. Despite these differences we each had a wonderful relationship with our children and had many happy times together as a family.

During these years of my practice I became involved in an unusual case involving a young pre-teen female. She was involved in a 4-wheel desert vehicle accident. I was called from surgery while she was undergoing an exploratory laparotomy because of intraabdominal injuries. The surgeons discovered that he urethra had been transected at the level of the bladder and was separated from the bladder. The bladder had retracted some distance from the urethra. This is a serious, uncommonly seen injury. The junction of the bladder and urethra is a sophisticated neuromuscular area which controls voiding and continence in the female. Rather than trying to repair that injury at the time I elected to put a tube in the bladder and return to that injury when all the adjacent areas were healed.

The question in this case was would that sophisticated neuromuscular junction of the bladder and urethra function properly when reattached? I was skeptical of this surgery working 100% percent of the time. Some other urologists estimated there was a less than 20% chance of that operation being successful. Several weeks later a friend of mine and I returned her to surgery and reattached the bladder to the urethra. After we removed the catheter from the bladder, the bladder worked perfectly. We were all overjoyed. She went on to have a normal life and at times returned to see me to tell me how she was doing.

This gives me the opportunity to tell you, on a much lighter note, about a problem that could develop in your marriage centering around your bladders. The male and female bladders behave much differently. In the male, the urine has to pass through the prostate before it exits by way of the urethra. The prostate offers some resistance to the flow of urine through it. In doing so and over time, the male develops a strong and muscular bladder. It can also fire off quickly. This translates into a voiding pattern in the male that is characterized by feeling of having to go soon after the sensation of a full bladder develops. Putting it another way, "when you have to go you have to go".

The situation is much different in the female. There is very little resistance between the bladder and urethra. She can go more easily and smoothly than her male counterpart. There is another component to her bladder. Her mother has always told her to try not to urinate in public restrooms. As she grows older she develops a thin walled bladder and can hold her urine in her bladder for long periods. Her bladder continues enlarge in size. She would never use a honey bucket (porta potty). Her bladder keeps growing in size and has the ability to hold large volumes for prolonged periods. She has developed the female "social bladder".

Now let's say these two different bladders get married and decide to drive New Mexico for their honeymoon. They are totally unaware that they are soon going to have the first major conflict in their marriage. As they near Albuquerque she is driving when he says, "I have to go". She says, "We only have 60 miles to go and you can hold if for another 60 minutes." Can you see where I'm going?

He responds, "What the hell are you talking about, I have to go now. Stop this car now!". This is the first real conflict of their marriage. She can't believe she married such a volatile person and he can't believe he married such a controlling person. Some couples will survive this initial conflict and go on to have a wonderful marriage. Some will not.

If this couple had just had the patience to wait until they both were over 70 years old. At that time, they both would be urinating frequently and they could even go to urinate together, further enhancing the bond of their marriage.

My next major bipolar issue occurred 4 years later. In those days, you did not need permission from a hospital committee to initiate a new type of treatment. I was going to use a new procedure to provide hyperalimentation for my patient. This new procedure was designed to provide calories and nutrients to patients whose bowels were not functioning after surgery (ileus). The system that I was going to employ was based on the principle of the fact that the first part of the small bowel (the jejunum) would absorb this hyperalimentation solution even if the bowel itself was non-functional.

The procedure was to pass a weighted, longer than normal, NG tube into the stomach and have it pass into the small bowel. After that I was going to deliver the hyperalimentation solution through this long NG tube into the small bowel. The drug company representative had already given me the hyperalimentation solution in a powder form. All you had to do was place the powder into hot water and then allow it to cool. It then could be passed into the small bowel by way of the NG tube, which had made it's way to that part of the small bowel. I made an error in judgment when I decided to make this solution in the kitchen area in the back of the ICU.

I explained to the nurses what I was doing. The nurses became concerned about what I was doing. The fact that they had not seen this being done before contributed to their concern. A nurse called my partner and asked him to get me out of there. My partner came and told me I had to get out of there because the nurse was upset with what I was doing. In retrospect, I can see why she felt that way. At the time I just wanted to provide my patient with hyper-alimentation, even though it was the first time it had been done in that hospital.

My partner told me he had to get me out of there. I told him I did not want to go. He said he was going to go get security to help him get me out of there. Oh my God! I could just see me being dragged out of this ICU by hospital security.

I then made, what in retrospect, was a stupid mistake. I decided to get out of there by another way. The ICU was on the second floor. I looked out the window and saw that it was no problem to get to the ground by using the first-floor awning. Remember, I had been up and down rope ladders in the mini boot camp I had gone through with the Marine Corps before going to Vietnam. Down I went with no problem.

Unfortunately, no one knew that. Because of that, the story was that Dr. Emery jumped out of a second story window. I certainly did not consider jumping out of a window. My partner must have been shocked to see that I was no longer there. He caught up to me outside and said I should go to the psychiatry unit to make sure I was ok. By that time, I had enough sense not to do another stupid thing to be uncooperative.

I went to the psychiatry unit and was seen by the psychiatrist there. He saw me and after a period of time the charge nurse came and told me I could go. A couple of days later I was suspended by the hospital. My suspension would be reversed if I consulted with a psychiatrist. I was to be reinstated to the staff after I completed at complete review by psychiatry.

In retrospect, there is no question in my mind that I had been in some degree of a hypomanic episode during the time that this incident occurred. The Chief of Staff of the other large hospital in the area met with me and said they had no problem with me continuing to work there. I was very reassured to hear that from him.

Then a strange thing happened. I was seeing a divorce lawyer who I was talking to about my wife and my problems with our marriage. I told him about what had happened.

He told me he knew what was wrong with me and gave me the name of a psychiatrist to see. Can you believe that? This lawyer was telling me what was wrong with me. He was right!

I saw the psychiatrist he recommended and he said I likely had bipolar disorder. He was very knowledgeable about bipolar disorder and had done research in that field. He suggested that I start on lithium and I should take a period of time off while we were adjusting my medication and discussing how I could manage this problem. I agreed.

I made plans to take several months off to make an initial exploration on how to manage the problem. I ended up taking about eight months off and did several things during that time. First, I tried to learn as much about this disease that I could. I started out with the book Mood Swings and went from there. Today I would suggest one start with Bipolar Disorder for Dummies. This can be a very enlightening book to read.

Secondly, I joined the diversion program for physicians in California. The program had just begun and was designed to help California doctors who were dealing with substance abuse problems. It is an example of the philosophy of the state of California. They wanted to attempt to help their doctors and medical providers (nurses, dentists, pharmacists, etc.) so they could continue to help the state with it's medical care. Other states may not have had such programs.

The program helped me a great deal by allowing me to share experiences and ideas with others who were trying to deal with major problems. We spent many hours discussing various topics that pertained to our problems. I stayed in that program for a year and it certainly helped me.

Thirdly, I took a course on geography at a Junior College. I truly enjoyed this course.

After many months, I decided to return to work and started a solo practice in the same part of the city. One of the surgeons there allowed me to operate with him to get me adjusted to doing surgery again. By coincidence he had severed with the same USMC unit in the states that I was stationed with in Vietnam.

Again, my practice developed quickly and I was going back to doing patient care and surgery. One of the excellent nephrologists in our area continued to send me his most difficult surgery cases to me.

In time, I accepted the position of Chief of Surgery at two of the hospitals where I was working. As Chief of Surgery you manage the surgical affairs of all surgery sub-sections such as general surgery, urology, ENT, cardiothoracic surgery and anesthesia. If a new policy or disciplinarily action are sent out, these actions are sent out under your name, as Chief of Surgery, even though you might not agree with the decision made by the committee. I will show you an example of this later in the book.

An unusual case I had during this period of time dealt with a fractured kidney. The patient was a young man who was an extra point kicker for our local State University. During a game, the snap was fumbled and he picked up the ball and began to run with it. Being a soccer player, he was not use to running with the ball. The defensive linemen hit him hard. Later, on the bench, he became dizzy and was sent to the closet hospital. An evaluation in the hospital showed he had a fractured kidney. I was called to see him. My evaluation showed that he had fractured kidney, which had stopped bleeding by that time.

I talked to his father and informed him we could operate on him now and possibly have to remove the kidney. The alternative was to follow him closely to see if he would stabilize and then have an extended period of rehabilitation and see if the kidney would function properly on its own.

His father was concerned about taking the chance of removing the kidney because his son wanted to try out for professional football. At the time, you could not play in the NFL if you had only one kidney. I told him I would try the plan of observation without doing surgery now. Of course, the case was written up in the leading city newspaper.

Then I got a call from another urologist in the city. Coincidently, he was the same doctor who was with the National Guard Unit years earlier in the Watts Riot of 1965 when I was at the Big County. I told him of my plan. I thought he might have some great idea. Instead of that, he simply said, "Good luck". Over the next day or so it became apparent that the patient was not going to stabilize well enough to avoid surgery.

A general surgery friend of mine and I were able to remove the damaged part of the kidney and were able to leave half of the kidney which was functioning well. He and his dad were overjoyed at the outcome. He got his chance at professional football. He played in the indoor football league, but did not make it to the NFL. He wrote the most wonderful letter thanking me for helping him to get to a chance to play professional football.

Later in my career I operated on the head coach of our NFL team (Chargers) for a medical problem. This was another huge coincidence of my life. This coach was actually one of the coaches at UCLA, when my friend and I went there on a recruiting trip in 1956. I did not tell him that because I was too busy praying that nothing would go wrong with the surgery I had done on him. He did well and was discharged soon after the surgery. He actually interviewed another well-known NFL coach for a job while he was in the hospital.

When you have bipolar disorder, you may not want to appear that you are too happy or that you are too sad. You may ask yourself, "Am I too happy, today?" You can develop a concern that you may be manifesting a significant change in mood. I think I have had those concerns on occasion.

As you may have deduced from my description of my first depression, it is very difficult for me to describe these profound swings of emotion seen in bipolar disorder to someone who has not experienced this phenomenon. I hope I'm putting into understandable words the feelings one can have while going through one of these bipolar disorder swings of emotion. The word spontaneous is important in my explanation. These swings of emotions can occur "out of the blue". Remember this is an alteration in brain chemistry. You clearly do not know how or why this chemical change happened. The real problem is you cannot stop the change in the emotional swing. It seems to overwhelm you quickly. It must be like a drug induced "trip". You are on the trip and cannot stop the emotion swing. It's like you were injected with a chemical agent that is producing the swing of emotion.

If you are on a "feel good" mood swing it is difficult for you to believe that there is something wrong with you. You are feeling too good for there to be something wrong with you. It must be the feeling the meth addict is looking for when they inject themselves.

I understand that methamphetamine addicted patients are the most difficult addicts to rehabilitate because they do not want to get rid of that feel good feeling they are use to getting with the use of their drug. For the bipolar patients, they also feel good. They appear to be very upbeat and they have boundless energy. The bipolar patient or the methamphetamine addict may disrupt a gathering of people or do some other type of negative behavior. He or she may do or say things you would not ordinarily do or say.

In my opinion and experience, the hypomanic episodes usually develop spontaneously. You may or may not be aware you are developing this episode. After I was trained to listen to my body I think that I could feel such an episode coming on fairly early in the development of it. I began to feel slightly intense and slightly anxious. In retrospect, friends have told me I was much more talkative than usual. I felt very good and would attempt to complete tasks I felt were important to me. I became an impulsive shopper. I would buy things that I already had simply to have a back-up item.

With me, these episodes would usually involve a separation from my wife. I would leave home and move to an apartment or on one occasion even bought a trailer at the beach. What I did after that varied a great deal. Remember all this time I was feeling very good and thought I was making good decisions.

These episodes were very traumatic for my wife and children. I don't think our children realized what was going on, but that didn't mean they weren't feeling the trauma of what was happening. I want to emphasize again that they are wonderful people and have great families. I give my wife a great deal of credit for holding our family together during these difficult times.

After these hypomanic episodes began to subside, I invariability would develop a period of guilt and depression. When I read about the Blitzkrieg soldiers of WW11, I realized that I was going through a type of withdrawal from a feel good chemical abnormality in my brain that was now changing into a chemical situation that brought on these withdrawal-like symptoms as I began to swing into a depression mode. This must be a similar feeling that the German soldiers felt when they were going through withdrawal from Pervitin.

It is very common that the bipolar patient does not seek treatment during periods of an upswing in emotions. For the patient who is not diagnosed or is not being followed by a medical professional this can be a very important time for the patient and even for those around him or her. Will their behavior result in them getting the correct diagnosis? If not, they may continue with their undiagnosed bipolar disorder and face more problems in the future.

My doctors and I tried to determine if there was a predictable cycling to my illness. As I discussed before, the bipolar patient may have a cyclical component to their illness. It could vary from being very frequent to being very infrequent. My cycling period varied at around several years or more (up to 10 years).

Lithium is a medication that is commonly used to treat bipolar disease. The effect of this drug is to dampen the severity of hypomanic episodes. For the bipolar patients, they will experience a suppression of their affect. They will be less spontaneous and dynamic as they had been before they started this drug. There have been a number of other drugs used to control this disease. The new anti-seizure drugs seem to have the most promise in achieving this goal.

Unfortunately, I was to experience the most serious side effect of taking lithium, which is renal failure. A small percentage of people taking this drug will develop chronic renal failure. The renal failure is secondary to interstitial nephritis. This is a disease in which all the components of the kidney slowly degenerate. The disease is slowly progressive and eventually destroys both kidneys. At that time, the patient will have to be treated with permanent dialysis or require a kidney transplant. Once this condition was diagnosed my doctors stopped the lithium and placed me on another drug used to treat bipolar disorder. Years later, God again was to intervene in my life when my daughter donated a kidney to me.

This is off the subject, but perhaps this would be a good time for me to tell you of a significant change that began happening in the delivery of medical treatment to our citizens around this time in my life.

Since the inception of medical care in our country the doctors and medical providers have delivered medical care to the patient by a one to one relationship. You had your personal doctor who was responsible for your basic medical care. You were referred to other specialty providers, who were best qualified to treat your more specialized problem. You felt you had a personal relationship with your health care providers. Over the past 30 years or so things have begun to change or undergo a transition in the delivery of medical care in our country.

Today many of you are in or may have always been in a HMO medical care system. You are in a large HMO health care group that takes care of hundreds or thousands of patients. You do have a primary care physician, but now he or she is in a large network of doctors who seem to practice with a set of pre-determined protocols. These protocols or patterns of care have been shown to be the best way to treat medical problems within the specific HMO and will be used to treat your specific problem.

These protocols will be the basis of your care. It may seem like you and your doctor have been left out of medical decisions with regard to your care. There seems to be a less personal relationship between you and your doctors.

In this type of care there are major differences when compared to our previous one to one health care system. Today, you may see a nurse practitioner or physician's assistant more often than you see a primary care physician. These professionals are trained in that specialty and are capable of caring for your basic needs. If you need more advanced care you will be referred to your primary care physician. This physician will then take over your care for your medical problem or this physician will refer you to a specialist within the HMO system. It's like you have an existing protocol already planned for your overall medical care. The Kaiser Health Plan, The VA Health Care Plan and other large governmental health care plans have used this type of structure long before it began to be applied to the general patient population.

Prior to the introduction of this wide spread use of the HMO systems you made a contract with your doctor. He or she was responsible for your care. If you needed surgery you made another contract with the surgeon. Other referral physicians established care for you in the same manner. You had your team of doctors. They had complete control of your treatment.

As doctors, we too had to change from considering our patient on a one to one relationship. In that type of care, we felt completely responsible for the care of that patient whether that be in primary care or our specific specialty practice. Yes, there were relatively small groups of doctors who would partner together within a group specialty. These doctors covered call for each other and were likely well known as a small group of competent doctors in the community.

There was a very personal relationship between the patient and their doctor. In general, doctor's assistants were not trained in basic medical care and were more responsible for assisting the doctor in minor procedures in the office. With regard to the referral system, doctors referred you to a doctor they knew well and knew were competent to care for your specialty problem. You, the patient, seemed to have more control over your health care. You could ask to be referred to a specific doctor or could request to be sent to a different doctor if you felt more comfortable with that doctor.

This type of medical care was the standard of care in the United States since medicine developed in our country.

It's little wonder that the patients and doctors had some difficulties adjusting to this new HMO system of care in this country that began developing roughly in the late 80's and beyond in our country.

Today, you make a contract with your HMO. The doctors work for the HMO. Your treatment will follow the guidelines of the HMO. If you have not been in an HMO system before, you may have some difficulty adjusting to this new system of care. There may be delays in being seen initially in this system. There may be long waits to see a referring physician. You do have the option to be seen in an acute care clinic or the emergency room if you are not doing well while waiting to be seen through a normal protocol system.

To put mildly, and as briefly as possible, the whole transition to this new type of medical care was and continues to be a period of adjustment for the patient and doctor. That doesn't mean it can't be done, it just means it will take time for the medical providers and patients to adjust to this new and unfamiliar medical care systems.

The driving force to implement this new system is to attempt to control the rising cost of health care delivery to the people of this country. It has the advantage of having all your doctors in one place. The billing system is uniform. The transfer of information among your doctors is much faster. You will have automatic accesses to ancillary medical treatment, such as physical therapy and cardiac rehab. You will gradually get use to the new system and see the advantages the system has.

The new doctors in our country are being taught to practice within this new system and they are enjoying the advantages the system has for them as well. Gone are the days when the doctors learned medicine through long grueling hours of studying and learning to practice their specialty for little or no pay. You clearly can learn and perform well when you have worked for long hours, but that may not be a necessary part of your experience in the future. The doctors will be very well trained and preform their jobs extremely well.

This transition to this new system of care will be further complicated by a national political system in which each political party is trying to develop a type of health care plan that will be best for all Americans. They hassle each other back and forth to come up with a plan that will work. They want this done quickly. They seem to think such a complicated transition could be planned in a week or so.

Despite the large number of difficulties associated with this transition to a new plan of medical care in this country, if it is the will of the leaders of our country and the will of the people it will be done. One thing I know is that the doctors and supportive medical personnel will be very well trained and they will provide excellent medical care. It's just going to be a matter of the patients and the doctors and the supporting personnel to get use to the mechanics of the new delivery system.

Doctors, because of the nature of their work, can encounter very unusual and, at times, very humorous events in their practice. In Urology, we are the group that have the most unusual sexually related cases. I would like to tell you of some of the unusual cases I have seen.

This first case is an example of such a case and could be called the "ring around the penis" case. I was called to the ER because there was patient there with a large edematous penis. I went to the emergency room and, sure enough, there was a man there with a massively swollen edematous penis.

As I talked with him, his story gradually evolved. He had heard that if you put a constricting rubber band or hard ring around the base of your penis before you had an erection, the constricting band would not allow the penis drain blood and you would have long lasting erection. The idea sounded good to him, but the word long lasting seemed a little optimistic and he definitely chose the wrong constricting device.

I guess he thought a stainless-steel ring would be a nice durable thing to use to block the blood outflow from the penis. In any event, he chose a 3/8-inch diameter stainless steel ring as his constricting device, which he placed at the base of his penis before the he had the erection. You may see where we are going? Yes, it worked very nicely for maintaining an erection. Unfortunately, he fell asleep after his sexual experience.

He was awakened by a terrible pain in his penis. When he looked down the whole penis was swollen and was a bluish red color. He decided to get that stainless-steel ring off the base of his penis. Not only could he not get it off, he could not even see the ring of steel because of the swelling. He correctly thought that if he did not get the ring off, the whole thing would eventually fall off, ring and all. That was definitely the correct projection for this problem.

In the emergency room, I quickly agreed with him that we had to get the ring off the base of his penis and it had to be under general anesthesia. There was a way to get the ring off by placing a concentric constricting wrap around the penis to get the swelling down and slip the ring off. If that did not work the ring would have to be cut with a diamond drilling bit used in orthopedics.

We did not have that bit in our hospital and were arranging to have him transferred to a hospital where they had the bit and could do the surgery, if necessary.

Apparently, someone had called the fire department to send out the "jaws of life" unit. A fireman came into the emergency room in a yellow raincoat carrying the tree foot long "jaws of life" cutter. Thankfully the patient did not have heart disease or he might have had a heart attack right then. The expression on this patient's face was classic as he thought this "jaws of life" cutter would be used to cut the ring off.

After that scary episode for him he was transferred to the other hospital and the surgery with the constricting compression worked and they did not have to cut the ring off with the diamond bit.

As you know most professional licensing requires a certain number of CME credits per year. I registered for a CME class about an ancillary use of testosterone to provide medical treatment for patients. I have chosen to refer to this conference as "the powerful pellet" conference.

When I got there, I realized it was a Gynecology conference on the use of testosterone for improvement of female sexuality in the area of sexual drive (libido). That was fine, I hadn't heard that subject discussed before.

The conference began with an in-depth discussion of the chemical structure of testosterone in the free and bound forms. All of the receptor sites were pointed out along with the effect that testosterone had on them. It was pointed out that testosterone increased your energy level and libido. It also promoted hair loss. It made it more likely that you would develop pimples on your face. Less likely, it might deepen your voice.

They then described a study that they had done to determine the effects of a new FDA approved product that was now available. The product was in the form of a pellet that could easily be placed beneath the skin, usually in the abdomen. The pellet contained a certain small dose of testosterone mixed with a form of estrogen. They had placed these pellets in a group of patients and then sent out a questioner asking what effects the treatment had on the patients. They said they were astounded by the good effects this product had on the patients.

The next part of the conference consisted of several women giving their testimony on what affect the pellet had on them. To put it mildly, they all were ecstatic over what effect the pellet had on them.

The first lady got up and said she didn't realize that these feelings had been missing in her all her life. She was overjoyed with how the pellet had affected her. She had experienced a modest increase in energy, but the most wonderful result was the effect that the pellet had on her libido. She said she was shopping in a grocery store one day and caught herself trying to pick up the box boy. She said she had to rush home and call her husband and say to him, "Henry, you get home here right now". She said Henry was as pleased with the results of the pellet as she was.

Another lady got up and said she did not care if her hair was falling out, that she was developing some small facial pimples or that her voice might eventually deepen, she was not going to stop using the pellet.

Another lady said how overjoyed she was with the results she got from taking the pellet. She said she spent considerable time at her book club telling her friends how wonderful this pellet was. She recommended to several of them that they should look into getting this pellet placed in them by their gynecologist.

Actually, the conference was quite informative and enjoyable. I don't know what ever became of the pellet's use in the practice of gynecology. I don't know whether they changed the dosage of testosterone in the pellet, banned the use of the pellet all together or what.

I will tell you of a case I treated that I doubt if any other urologist has ever seen. You remember the case of the football place kicker who ruptured his kidney in a football game. Well, this next case involved a ruptured kidney. In this case the mechanism of injury to the kidney was quite different.

I was called to the emergency room to see a female patient with a traumatic rupture of her kidney. She had presented to the ER with abdominal pain and dizziness. The ER doctor did an extensive work-up and found that she had a ruptured kidney. She had been given blood and fluids, but was still unstable. When I talked to her and examined her I could see no other signs of blunt force trauma in the area of that kidney. I asked her what had happened.

She told me that the only thing she had done was to have extended and rough intercourse about 30 minutes before she began to feel pain and dizziness and went to the emergency room.

This would be more likely to happen if she had a kidney deformed by a tumor or cystic disease. The CT scan did not show evidence of either of these problems.

Her clinical course remained unstable and I informed her that we needed to operate on her to stop the bleeding and repair the kidney. If the bleeding could not be stopped or if the kidney could not be repaired, we would have to remove the kidney. She agreed to the surgery.

The kidney could not be salvaged at surgery and the kidney had to be removed. The patient recovered well and was discharged from the hospital on a normal recovery plan. I told her how sorry I was that this had happened to her. She said, "Don't worry, Doc, it was worth it".

I mentioned in the introduction to this book that when the patient with bipolar disorder has a hypomanic episode their behavior will be much more visible to the public than when they have a significant depressive swing in their emotional system.

Recall my example of the local banker who decided to direct traffic around an automobile accident. His intentions may have been good but his behavior and appearance were abnormal. I mentioned that these were the times when a hypomanic bipolar patient can draw the attention of the police or may put himself or herself into a position where they or someone else is in peril.

I described the hypomanic episode I had when I bought a trailer at the beach and confronted the man about the tire. During that same episode I went to a bar in a nearby city. This bar was frequented by military people from a local USMC base. I was going around the bar talking to the people from the base. I decided to play some pool. I went to the pool table and signed up for the next opening. After playing a while I had a verbal altercation with a young man playing against me. The conversation altercation escalated quickly and the young man pulled a straight razor out of his pocket and threatened me. Fortunately, I had enough sense to apologize and talk my way out that situation.

Had he pulled that razor out where there weren't other people around who knows what would have happened? Here I am again demonstrating what can easily happen when a bipolar patient is in the accelerated behavior of a hypomanic phase of their disease.

Try to imagine some of the embarrassing or dangerous situations you might get into during one of these major swings of emotion you could have if you were to have this disease.

How many of these major swings have I had during the forty years I have been treated for bipolar disease? I had three major depression reactions and three to four periods of hypomania. During that time, I have had less severe minor swings of emotion. Most of the time I remained the upbeat and friendly person I have always been.

I experienced my second major depression about 10 or 12 years after my first major depression. I was on my medicine as prescribed and was seeing my doctor routinely. This was going to be a classic breakthrough depression.

There was a medication that urologists were using to treat cancer of the prostate. It was originally used to treat non-localized cancer of the prostate. Some centers were using it earlier and earlier in the course of this cancer. I was following this course of treatment for my patients. I began to feel that I was using this medication wrong. I wasn't actually using it in a way that was wrong, but I thought I might be. This relative minor question of my treatment plan was the focus that was associated with a rapid and significant paranoia and depression. I saw my doctor. We decided to put me in the hospital. I took a leave of absence from the office and was admitted.

This depression, like the first one, was overwhelmingly severe. I was about to go through those severe and frightening symptoms again. I again lost all my coping skills as I got more depressed. There was that sick and painful feeling returning. This feeling lasted and worsened. Again, I went to work shops and meetings but continued to feel the same way.

I spent two to three weeks in the hospital with this depression. Again, I had no coping skills to apply to my condition. I was very malleable and was easy to manipulate in one direction or another. I went to meetings with other patients on the ward. These meetings did not help me in any way. I know the staff there was excellent, but it seemed as if my depression was unreachable for their efforts. Remember, I'm discussing this depression now. I could have never have written anything like this when I was in the midst of the depression. After two weeks in the hospital I was released.

With time and good treatment, I recovered from this depression. If you have gone through one of these depressions, you will never again fail to realize that a person with a disability is trying to manage their life as best they can.

Once I recovered from this second depression episode I returned to practice. Once again, my performance and results in patient care had not been diminished by this disease. It would be another 15 yrs before I developed another severe depression, which occurred after my renal transplantation.

Now, I would like to discuss an important issue for those who have, in particular, a mental disability. There are times in the workplace or in social situations where having that disability might be used against you.

I have been extremely lucky in my life to have a wonderful group of friends. I know that none of them would consider using the diagnosis of bipolar disorder against me. There has been an odd friend or two who were not too congenial and would occasionally not be accepting of my diagnosis. Of course, that is a very unpleasant experience for the person with the disability. The offended is likely to take offender off his or her favorite friend list.

The work place can be an entirely different situation. There may be those who you encounter in the workplace who will try to use a feature of your persona against you to gain some advantage for themselves. Surely most of us have experienced this activity during our lives. Jealously is the most common force driving such a person to use a feature of your persona against you.

This type of action can take many forms. Are there fellow workers jealous of you because you are too attractive? Are you so good at your job that you might generate ire in a fellow employee? Is your personality too effervescent and friendly to others that you might create jealously in a workmate? Are you simply standing in the way of a jealous person trying to move up the ladder?

Surely these are not uncommon problems we all can face in the workplace. Having a disability might make this part of your persona easier to take advantage of than some of the other parts of your persona.

Do I think I have encountered such incidents in my life. Yes, and for more parts of my persona than just having a disability. It's just that if you have a disability, it is easier to get at you by someone who is jealous of something you are doing. In the workplace I have not been a jealous person. I certainly have admired those who are better at something than I am.

At one point during my practice I was asked to join a group of four urologists. I was happy to join them. I was working hard with our patients. It began to appear that the leader or the group was the only one in the group who could make decisions for the rest of the group. I met with him one day and he asked me why I hadn't done this procedure on a patient. The procedure was contraindicated in that patient and I told him so. He got very upset.

Not long after that he wrote a letter to another hospital saying that he and the group would no longer take call with me because of my behavior. I wasn't aware of any abnormal behavior I was exhibiting. Apparently, by referring to my behavior he was implying that my bipolar disorder had become unstable and that accounted for my comments to him. None of my friends had brought that up to me. I met with a committee at the other hospital and after talking with me for two meetings they decided I was fine. This was an example of where my disability was used against me in the workplace.

I initiated a legal proceeding against this urologist for initiating an unjustified defamation against me. The proceeding was settled in my favor. To me, this urologist had used my diagnosis in an effort to defame my character. I took this issue to an independent group legal persons and they concluded that he had acted inappropriately. He was instructed to write me a letter of apology and to pay for the cost of the lawyers involved.

Some time later, I was acting as the Chief of the Urology Subsection of the hospital. The urologist, who had written the letter to the other hospital about me, suggested that the urologists in our hospital stop taking call in the emergency room. He thought the hospital could hire some urologist or group of urologists to take call in our ER. I was against this idea because it ran the risk of leaving our ER devoid of on-call urologists to help them. One of the urologists on the committee said I was too altruistic.

A friend of mine and I volunteered to take the ER call until a decision was made by the hospital administration about the call system. The administration decided that our hospital urologists should resume the call.

Some time after that incident, I was called to see the Chief of Staff and one other member of the executive committee. The Chief of Staff began the meeting by saying that I was summarily suspended from the staff. This statement was a total shock to me. I asked him why?

He said someone had reported me because of having abnormal behavior when I gave the hospital operators a gift. He said that I had given them a small bag of sweet rolls. They said that there were packets of sugar and containers of cream in the bag. They were very offended. Some of the operators were overweight and they thought I was making fun of them suggesting that they put cream and sugar on the rolls.

I told them I would never try to embarrass them under any circumstances. I knew the Chief of Staff was going be embarrassed when I told him what had happened and how the gift had gotten there.

That day, I was in another hospital not too far away. I picked up some rolls and coffee for the x-ray tech and nurse in the ESWL ("stone busting") trailer. I put cream and sugar packets in the bag with the rolls in case either of them wanted cream or sugar for their coffee.

I found out that the ESWL trailer was not there that day. I poured the coffee out of the cups. Then I decided to take the rolls to this hospital and give them to one of the groups of nurses or hospital personnel. When I went into the hospital I saw the women in the hospital operator section. I went up to the window and told them I had brought them a treat. They thanked me.

The Chief of Staff looked very surprised after I explained what had happened. I think he realized what a mistake had been made. When I brought the rolls to the operators in this hospital, they felt insulted because of the cream and sugar containers were in the bag with the rolls. Clearly, they had no idea that I had gotten the rolls for the people in the ESWL trailer at the other hospital. I could understand why they wondered why the packets of sugar and the little containers of cream were in there. It was simply a misunderstanding.

Apparently, someone had told the executive committee of the hospital of this incident. Presumably the committee saw this as an indication that I was having a period if instability of my bipolar disorder. For a suspension to get to this point it has to be discussed by the 10 to 12 doctors on the committee. They would have to be convinced that a suspension was warranted. The whole situation was baffling to me.

I told them the whole thing was a misunderstanding. I was sorry for that. I was very busy and had to get back to my patients in the hospital. They said that they were having another meeting in a week. I told them that I had to see my hospitalized patients in the morning. I needed an answer on this whole matter in the morning.

The Chief of Staff called me the next day and told me that I was no longer suspended. Apparently, the previous Chief of Staff called my doctor and asked him how I was doing. My doctor indicated that he thought I was fine.

I am pointing out this incident as an example of how your disability can be used against you in the workplace. Someone or some group of people apparently had used this incident to say that I was having some instability with regard to my bipolar disorder.

The Chief of Staff called me later and apologized for what had happened. He was very upset to have been put in the place where he had to inform me of the suspension. I thanked him and told him that I was familiar with the system. When you are leader of a committee you have to carry out the desires or decisions of the committee even through you may not agree with them. I understand he took a period of time off work after this incident.

In my experience, some of the physician political leaders in our hospitals and medical organizations are self-appointed and have self-interests other than the basics of medicine and good patient care. They are in the minority in our profession. I have seen these self-serving political physicians try to impede or even destroy another physician's career. Hopefully, this small group of deranged physicians will disappear from our medical communities in the future.

In relation to this type political maneuvering, two of my physician friends say publicly that I saved their lives. These doctors had incurred the ire of some unethical doctors, who, in turn, were determined to hurt or destroy their careers.

One of these urologists I helped came to our community from another state. He had been working with a new and unproven diagnostic tool for detection of cancer of the prostate. He was given a cold reception by the 50 or so urologists in our county. He was given the impression by them that if this diagnostic procedure did not work they would discredit him greatly. One disjointed urologist even said he knew where his family lived. This new urologist looked like a lonely man on the night of one of our county meetings.

For the rest of the time I knew this urologist I helped him with his decisions on treatment for his patients. I helped him with any surgery he needed help with. We helped each other with emergencies. For the rest of the time I stayed the city he use to introduce me as "The man who saved his life". I mean he even introduced me like that to prominent urologists from other parts of the country.

There was another urologist in our part of the city who said I saved his life. He was saying publicly that he had been stabbed in the back by a former partner (it happened to be the urologist who had earlier had tried to defame me). Seemingly, he and this partner had a social or economic difference which had driven them apart. Suddenly my friend was on his own. He was the best young urologist in our community and had done some significant research in our specialty.

His older partner had basically deserted him and tried to discredit and destroy him. This older partner seemed to be developing a pattern of trying to hurt other doctors in the community.

This young urologist was my friend and I asked him to call me any time he needed help. I also told him I would cover him any time he needed it and I would take call for him anytime. He also would say to me and others that I had saved his life. I was actually grateful for the opportunity to help him.

I was always so happy and proud of the fact that some of the nurses would call me if they needed help. I was glad to help them even if some of the problems they asked me to help them with were not in my field. I can tell you that the nurses are the backbone of our profession and to try to help them should be regarded as an honor for we physicians.

One night, I got a call in the middle of the night from one of the nurses at the hospital. She apologized for calling me and told me that she knew I was not on call, but she wondered if I could help her with a patient. I sure could. She told me that she had a post-op patient who was bleeding from his Foley catheter and that the patient's blood pressure was very low.

Apparently, she had called the on-call doctor who was responsible for his care and told him of the problem. This doctor said he could not see the patient because he had socio-economic differences with the patient's primary urologist. I had never heard anything like that. Could an on-call physician responsible for the patient's care actually say that?

I told her that I would be there in 10 to 15 minutes. I asked her to get some equipment for me. On the way to the hospital I called the anesthesiologist of call and said that I might need a central venous line on the patient. When I got there, I treated the patient by freeing his bladder of clots. The anesthesiologist started an appropriate IV solution and later gave the patient blood. We transferred the patient to the ICU. The bleeding stopped.

Soon after that I operated on the patient when the bleeding recurred. I then transferred the case back to his original urology group. The patient did eventually recover, although he had a stroke during his recovery process. The family thanked me for my help. They said they were just happy that he recovered and they had him at home.

It was obvious that such an incident should be investigated by the hospitals committee system. I presented this case to the surgical committee for review. I simply wanted to know what factors in our hospital had developed that would allow this type of treatment to occur.

I was shocked and bewildered when the Chief of Surgery told me that the case was designated as being within the standard of care for the hospital. Was he serious! No hospital that I had been in would ever call that case within the standard of care.

Clearly this was a major and serious difference of opinion between me and the Chief of Surgery. I couldn't' imagine that the committee could make such a decision.

Not long after that I was told that my cases were to be reviewed by the State of California. I asked why the committee had decided they wanted my cases to be reviewed by the state. I got no answer. The whole thing didn't make any sense. I may have had the best surgical outcomes in the hospital. I had no operative or post-operative deaths or many significant complications from my surgeries. I thought it possibility could have something to do with my strong disagreement with the decision of the committee.

Despite that, I prepared to my cases to be reviewed. The rules of the review were that the two reviewing state sponsored urologists who I was to meet with would not have any advance knowledge of any of my cases.

When I met with the two urologists representing the State of California, the older of the two said, "What the hell are we doing here". This remark was probably because of the few number problems I had during the year when I had done 300 surgeries. I told him I was not told why this review was being done. He said he did not know why either.

Shortly after that he said, "Tell me about the case where a patient had bladder bleeding while recovering from surgery." Why was this reviewing urologist asking me about this case, when I was told that the condition of the review was that the reviewing doctors would not have any advance knowledge of any of the cases I had done. This was a clear violation of the conditions that I was told were in place for the review. Despite my feelings, I decided to complete the process of the review. We then reviewed the cases I was asked to review. This involved reviewing a random sampling of 300 surgeries I had done during that year.

After the review, the younger of the reviewing urologists told me that I was a great urologist and he hoped that his children would have the same dedication to their job as I did. This was very nice to hear. He recommended that I should not try to do everything myself and rely more on the consulting specialists around me. I clearly understood this recommendation and appreciated it. I put that recommendation into practice. I never found out why the review had been requested.

Within a few months of these events happening I decided to take a position in a cancer treatment center in southern

Arizona. It had been a few years since I had any uncontrollable major swings of emotion. During that time, I was in close contact with my doctors. While in Arizona I established a contact with a psychiatrist there. I enjoyed my time there and worked with many good doctors in that area.

Near the end of my career I returned to California and took a job to provide urologic care for two hospitals in northern California. I did multiple surgeries in these hospitals and had no significant problems except for a complication of a post-operative abdominal wall cellulitis in a patient who I had placed a suprapubic tube into the bladder. I had not placed this patient on a broad enough spectrum of antibiotics to prevent the development of the cellulitis.

In one of these hospitals, things did not go well from the beginning. I was working in an employed position in a new hospital clinic there. The medical director of the clinic criticized my record keeping. I was using a system which I had been using for years. Things went from bad to worse. For my part, I was very reactive to their criticism and was not hesitant to tell them so. I certainly contributed to the fact that things did not go well at that hospital.

On a positive note, I introduced the use of the holmium laser to treat kidney stones in this county in northern California. Unfortunately, the holmium laser was located in the second hospital I was covering. This meant that I had to transfer patients to that hospital to treat their stones with the laser. The people of this hospital were not pleased with that situation

I did get a commendation letter from a patient thanking me for treating him at 3 o'clock in the morning for an acute urologic problem. His urologist in another city also wrote me a letter of thanks.

One day in the operating room a male operating room nurse became very angry and behaved very badly when I asked him a question during the surgery. Everyone in the room was surprised by his behavior. I tried to talk to him after the incident, but he refused to talk to me.

After that, I resigned my position there as a hospital employed urologist and concentrated my urologic care on patients in the second hospital in the county. The first hospital then filed a suspension notice for me.

I discussed the complete experience I had had with this hospital with a representative from the Medical Board of California. We had a long discussion of what had happened there. I acknowledged that I had not handled the whole experienced as well as I could have. The board took no action against me. They were critical of the fact that had not handled the case of the patient who developed the cellulitis well as I could have. I agreed with them.

My experience at the other hospital in that area was very good. The hospital is under a large health care system and was well run. I introduced the use of the holmium laser for the treatment of kidney stones in that hospital. We did a lot of successful treatment of kidney stones there.

My final assignment was to help out in a very good District Medical Center in western Kansas. This medical center was excellent and the doctors there were excellent. I really enjoyed working there.

During these years I continued to monitor my disease closely and keep in contact with of my doctors. I saw other psychiatrists when I was in Arizona and Kansas. I appreciated them helping with my problem. They were wonderful doctors. I had no recurrences of significant mood swings during those years.

The thing I am most proud of during my career was the fact that I maintained steadfastly that the principle of good patient care and safety was the single most important part of medicine. I'm certainly in the good company with the overwhelming majority of doctors in our country.

I am very proud of the fact that nurses would call me if they needed help with some of their patients. I hope I never forget that the nurses are the cog of the wheel that propels the discipline of medicine forward.

During the time since I was diagnosed as having bipolar disorder, I have experienced many of the different scenarios one can have with this disease.

The best thing I did was to acknowledge that I had this disease. The next best thing I did was to follow the treatment plan that my doctors outlined for me. Despite doing these things, I experienced some breakthrough exacerbations of the disease. Bipolar disorder patients should be aware that this can happen and be prepared to deal with these breakthroughs as best as they can.

Do I think I handled this disease as well as I could? In terms of my profession, yes. I followed the guidance of my doctors, stopped drinking alcohol entirely, did not miss taking medicine, listened to my body and took time off when I thought my medical decisions could be affected by this disease. Because of this I was fortunate enough to never have had a negative patient care outcome because of this disease.

In my personal and social life, there are many things I could have done better. Had I done better in this phase of my life, I could have reduced the hurt and disappointment I caused the people around me.

I believe one of the most important things we can do in understanding and dealing with this disease is to communicate with each other and share our experiences.

There are national organizations dealing with depressive diseases. I think it would be beneficial to develop more local organizations under the supervision of local psychiatrists, psychologists or nurse practitioners. In my opinion, these local organizations would be more comfortable for patients and their families.

Thank you for sharing this book with me. I have enjoyed sharing with you what I know about this disease and how it affected my life.

My overall message, as a patient, is that if you have this disease: Acknowledge you have this disease; Seek out good professional care; Follow your treatment plan religiously; Take your medication as directed; Do not, under any circumstances, engage in any substance abuse; Try to get into a group of people with this disease and share experiences with them; Look forward to the fact that you have a good outlook for a productive and enjoyable life.

One final thought is to not let someone's opinion of your disability stand in the way of your dreams or life goals. They are not the one living inside you.

The best for you always,

John

Index

A

Aborigines 82, 84-5
  initiation ritual of 84
American Civil War 42, 46-8, 53, 59
amphetamine 13, 17, 29
anesthesia 44-5, 91, 115, 129, 167, 217, 229

B

Barnes, Bill 96
Barry, John 150, 183-4, 188
Battle of Antietam 44
Battle of El Alamein 17
Benzedrine 17
betel nut 124, 167
bipolar disease 2-3, 7-8, 10-11, 13, 22-4, 27-30, 34, 37, 204, 209, 216, 223, 234
  classifications 10
bladder, social 212
Blake, Dean 65
Blitzkrieg 14, 20
blunt trauma 104, 203, 232
Boone, Daniel 42, 196

Brown, Joe E. 86

C

Camp Las Pulgas 146, 148
Camp Pendleton 68, 146
Cannon, Billy 73
Carmen, Charles 113
Charleston ix, 34-5, 38, 40, 42, 49-50, 56-7, 59, 63-6, 109, 210
Charleston High School 63, 65
Churchill, Winston 10
chylothorax 137-8
Coal River 50, 55
Comroe, Julius 112
Confederate army 43
Continuing Medical Education (CME) 230

D

Davis, Ernie 109-10
Dean River 196, 198
Democratic National Convention 126, 178
Dempsey, Jack 35, 56

depression 2, 6-7, 10, 13-14, 16, 18, 21-2, 25-6, 29, 37, 39, 205-9, 221, 234-6
  bipolar 6-7, 26, 205
  episodes of 2, 7, 18, 27, 209, 236
  first major 25, 235
  nonchemical 6
  second major 236
  severe 7, 10, 14, 21, 25, 37, 207
Deschutes River 192
dopamine 11-13, 25
Drake, Ducky 90, 110
Dunphy, J. Englebert 113
DuPont 49

E

Edelman, Isidore 112, 121
electrolyte abnormality *see* hypernatremia 102
euphoria 2, 13, 20, 24, 204

F

Ferris, Jessie 35, 56
First Hospital Company 168-9
flu epidemic 87
fluid loss 101
Foley, Frederic 189
Foley catheter 124, 189, 244
football ix, xiv, 35, 57-9, 61-4, 73-4, 85-6, 90, 92-3, 96-100, 104-10, 199-200, 203, 218-19, 232
  professional 64, 109, 200, 203, 218-19
  youth 108

G

German army 14
ginseng 47-8
Gotch, Frank 112-13

H

head injuries 104-5
health maintenance organization (HMO) 224-6
Hillenbrand, Laura 76
Hitler, Adolf 15, 17, 75
holmium laser 247-8
hospital ships 154
house call service 140, 144
Huggins, Charles 182
hydration 103
hyperactivity 2, 13, 21-2
hyperalimentation 213-14
hypernatremia 102
hypomania 4, 10-11, 13, 16, 19-21, 24, 234

I

illness, depressive 206-7
immunosuppression 186-7
induction course 146, 149

J

Jackson, Thomas "Stonewall" 46
Jolie, Angelina 76

K

Kanawha River 34, 40, 49-50, 68
Kennedy, John F., death of 120, 153, 178
Kennedy, Robert 126, 178

King, Martin Luther, Jr. 126
Knife and Gun Club 135
Kobiashia, Steve 70, 114
Ky Hoa 157, 172

L

Lamictal 21
Letterman, Jonathan 44
Letterman Hospital 45
Lincoln, Abraham 10
lithium 19, 21, 31, 216, 223
Los Angeles County Hospital ix, 25, 36, 128, 130-2, 134, 139, 141, 144-5, 201
lysergic acid diethylamide (LSD) 119

M

marijuana 29, 48
Mays, Willie 56
Medical Board of California 248
medical internship 36, 123, 128, 138, 140, 151
mental disease 1-2
methamphetamine 13, 15-17, 19, 24, 220
  crystal 13, 19
military hospitals 155
Morell, Theodor 15, 17
Mr. Moto (wrestler) 88-9

N

National Basketball Association (NBA) 65
nephrectomy 186-7
  bilateral 186-7
Nimpo Lake 199

O

overheating 98, 101
overhydration *see* water intoxication 103

P

pacification program 156-7, 168
paranoia 6, 13-14, 16, 25, 204, 235
patient care 28, 38, 123, 140, 153, 186, 209, 217, 236, 249
  good 28, 209, 242, 249
Pervitin 14-18, 20, 222
Phi Delta Theta Fraternity 73, 86
physiology
  fluid and electrolyte 98, 103, 112, 121
  lung 112
Pickwickian Syndrome 121
Presley, Elvis 35, 63
prisoner of war (POW) camps 46-7, 179
private practice 37, 190, 201

R

Reynolds, Bill 76
ROK (Republic of Korea) Marines 152, 169

S

San Francisco County Hospital 120, 123
Sanders, Red 73, 85, 96
Sebastian, Tony 33
serotonin 11-13, 25
Shire, Tom 153
Shultz, Earl 64, 113-14
Smith, Chris 65

Smith, Skip   73, 89
South Charleston   40, 49
South Vietnam   119, 151-2, 156-7, 174, 179
splenectomy   187
sports medicine   90-1, 101
Starr, Al   185
steroids   97, 106
subsistence farmers   35, 60-1
suffocation   120
suicide   3, 7, 17, 205
surgeries
 general   48, 70, 134, 185, 217
 imaginative   85
 primitive   47, 83-4

T

Tet Offensive   xi, xiv, 25, 37, 126, 160, 174, 178
therapy   21-2, 31, 206, 208, 226
 group   206-8
Torrance   ix, 35, 38, 66-71, 73-6, 201
Torrance High School   67-8, 72, 74-5, 201
transplant service   188
transplantation   185-8
 kidney   37, 186, 204
 renal   185, 187
transurethral resection of the prostate (TURP)   189

U

Unbroken (Hillenbrand)   76
Union Army   43-4
Union Carbide   40, 49, 60, 65, 67
United States Army   44, 156, 172

United States Marine Corps   145-6, 151-2, 217, 234
University of California–San Francisco School of Medicine   3, 33, 103, 131, 153, 201
University of Oregon Medical School   37, 74, 150, 182, 184, 190
University of Oregon Medical School Hospital   37

V

Van Gaulder, Gary   74, 184
Vietnam   26, 37-8, 47, 81, 121, 126, 133, 139, 145-53, 155-7, 168, 174-5, 177-80, 183, 201
Vietnam War   ix, xi, xiv, 26, 37-8, 121, 126, 139, 145, 154, 175, 178, 201

W

Watts   131-3
Watts Riots   36, 126
Weil, Max   153
West, Jerry   64, 114
West Point   108
Williams, Andy   203
World War II   10, 14, 18, 40, 81

Z

Zamperini, Louis   35, 74-5

www.ingramcontent.com/pod-product-compliance
Lightning Source LLC
Chambersburg PA
CBHW030311080526
44584CB00012B/522